Rea

- Descriptions in this manual are based on what is available as at the time of writing this guide, and it may not be 100% accurate again if there is a major software update to iPhone 8, iPhone 8 Plus, or iPhone X.

- Depending on your local network service provider or your location, some of the features discussed in this guide may not be available on your iPhone 8, iPhone 8 Plus, or iPhone X.

- All information supplied in this guide is for an educational purpose only and users bear the responsibility for using it.

- Although I took tremendous effort to ensure that all information provided in this guide are correct, I will welcome your suggestions if you find out that any information provided in this guide is inadequate or you find a better way of doing some of the actions mentioned in this guide. All correspondences should be sent to pharmibrahimguides@gmail.com

Copyright and Trademarks

iPhone 8, iPhone 8 Plus and iPhone X are trademarks of Apple, Inc. All other trademarks are the property of their respective owners. Reproduction of this book without the permission of the owner is illegal. Any request for permission should be directed to **pharmibrahimguides@gmail.com**.

About This Guide

Finally, a simplified guide on iPhone 8, iPhone 8 Plus and iPhone X is here– this guide is indeed a splendid companion for these high-end phones.

This is a very thorough, no-nonsense guide, useful for both experts and newbies. This guide contains a lot of information on iPhone 8, iPhone 8 Plus and iPhone X.

It is full of actionable steps, hints, notes, screenshots and suggestions. This guide is particularly useful for newbies/beginners and seniors. Nevertheless, I strongly believe that even the techy guys will find some benefits reading it.

Enjoy yourself as you go through this very comprehensive guide.

PS: Please make sure you do not give the gift of iPhone 8, iPhone 8 Plus or iPhone X without giving this companion guide alongside with it. This guide makes your gift a complete one.

Table of Contents

How to Use This Guide (Please Read!)

This guide is an unofficial manual of iPhone 8, iPhone 8 Plus and iPhone X and it should be used just as you use any reference book or manual.

To quickly find a topic, please use the table of contents. This will allow you to quickly find information and save time.

When I say you should carry out a set of tasks, for example when I say you should tap **Settings >Sound> Notifications & actions**, what I mean is that you should tap on **Settings** and then tap on **Sound**. And lastly, you should tap on **Notifications & actions**.
When a function is enabled, the status switch will appear bold and colored. On the other hand, when a function is disabled, the status switch will appear gray.

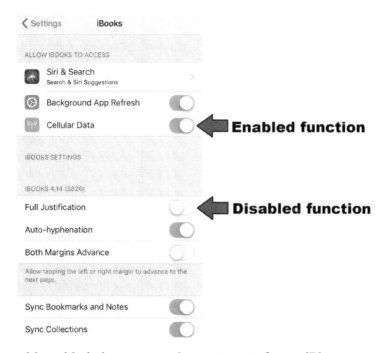

I hope this guide helps you get the most out of your iPhone.

Getting Started With Your iPhone

Unpacking Your Device

When you unpack your product box, check your product box for the following items:

1. iPhone 8, iPhone 8 Plus or iPhone X
2. EarPods with Lightning Connector
3. Lightning to 3.5 mm Headphone Jack Adapter
4. Lightning to USB cable
5. USB Power Adapter
6. Eject Pin (the eject pin is located on one of the quick start guides)   No
7. Quick Start Guides

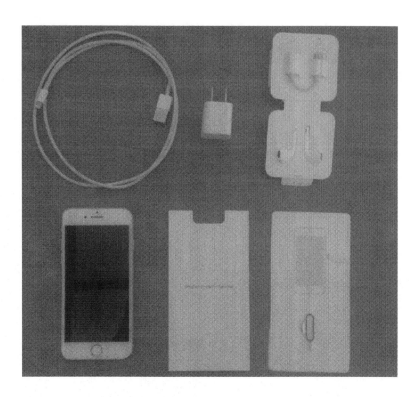

Inserting a SIM Card

1. While the phone is off, insert the SIM ejection tool into the SIM tray eject hole and push until the tray pops out. Please note that you may need to apply force for the SIM tray to pop out. The SIM ejection tool is included in iPhone's box.

**SIM Tray
Eject Hole**

**SIM
Ejection
Tool**

2. Place the SIM Card into the tray with the metal contacts facing down.

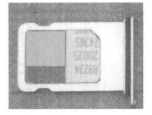

3. Insert the SIM Card tray into the phone and push until it locks into place

4. Press and hold the Power Button to turn the phone on.

Please note that iPhone 8, iPhone 8 Plus or iPhone X uses Nano SIM. In addition, you don't need to turn off your phone before you remove the SIM Card.

Turning Your Phone on and off

Just like many other smartphones, turning on your device is as simple as ABC. To turn on your phone, press and hold the Side button. If you turn on your phone for the first time, follow the on-screen instructions to set it up.

Side Button

To turn off your phone, press and hold the side button and then drag the slider.

To switch off iPhone X, press the volume up button and the side button at the same time. Then drag the slider that appears.

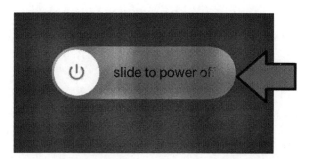

Please do not vex if you find it unnecessary reading about how to turn on/off your device. I have included it, in case there may be someone reading this guide who is a complete novice and knows close to nothing on smartphones.

Note: Please note that you will need your Apple ID to setup your device. If you are using an iPhone for the first time and you don't have an Apple ID, you may create one whenever you're asked to sign in by clicking account creation button.

Tips:

- Some network provider may require you to enter a PIN when you switch on your phone. You can try entering **0000 or 1234.** This is the default PIN for many network providers. If you have a problem entering the correct PIN, please contact your network service provider.

- During the setup, you may skip a process by tapping **SKIP/Not Now**. Usually, you will have the option to perform this process in the future by going to your phone settings.

- If you are upgrading from an iPhone to iPhone 8, you will have the option to restore your backups to your iPhone 8 during the phone setup.

- While using your phone for the first time, you should have the option to transfer your contents from your old Android phone to iPhone 8, iPhone 8 Plus or iPhone X. Just carefully follow the onscreen instructions to do this. Please note that if you skip this process during the setup, you may not be able to use this process of file transfer again unless you want to **erase your iPhone** (please see page 217 to learn more about this) and start over. To learn more about this process of file transfer, please see page 19.

- It is likely that your phone will consume a large amount of data during the phone setup, I will advise that you connect to a wireless network if you can. Using a mobile network during the setup may be expensive.

- When you start using your phone, you may probably notice that your phone screen locks within few seconds after you finish interacting with it. To allow your phone stay longer before it locks, change the Auto-lock setting. To do this:

  - From the Home screen, tap the Settings icon .
  - Scroll down and tap **Display & Brightness**.
  - Tap on **Auto-Lock**. Then choose an option.

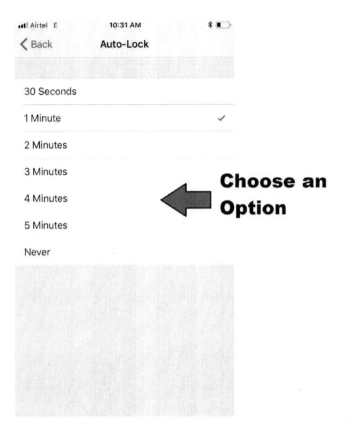

Please note that selecting a longer timeout may make your battery discharge faster.

- *Do you need to charge your phone before first use?*

To the best of my knowledge, it is not necessary. If you charge it before first use, that is cool. But if there is no way to charge it, then you can use it straightaway without charging it. I have learnt that the new lithium batteries used in smartphones don't really need to be charged before first use (provided that the battery still has power).

Get to know your device

Device Layout

Please note that iPhone 8 and iPhone 8 Plus look very similar except that iPhone 8 Plus is bigger and has two back cameras. In the picture shown below, I have used iPhone 8 as an example. On the other hand, iPhone X lacks a dedicated Home button and also has two back cameras.

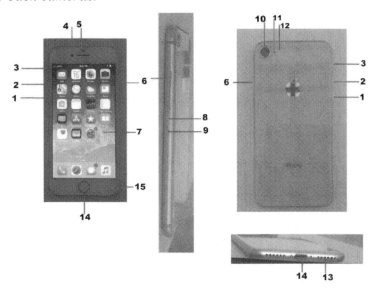

Number	Function
1.	Volume Down Button
2.	Volume Up Button
3.	Ring/Silent Button
4.	Front Facing Camera
5.	Receiver/front Microphone
6.	Side Button
7.	Touch Screen
8.	SIM card tray
9.	SIM Ejection Hole
10.	Back Camera
11.	Rear Microphone
12	Flash
13.	Built-in stereo speakers
14.	Lightning connector port
15.	Home button/Touch ID Sensor

Get to Know the Settings Tab

I am talking about the Settings tab under this section because I will be referring to this tab a lot.

The Settings tab has many subsections and because of this, I will advise that you use the Search menu (denoted by the lens icon) to quickly find what you are looking for.

To access the Settings menu, from the Home screen, tap **Settings** .

Then tap on the search icon (located at the top of the screen) and type a keyword corresponding to the settings you are looking for. For example, if you are looking for settings relating to battery, just type **Battery** into the search bar. The result filters as you type.

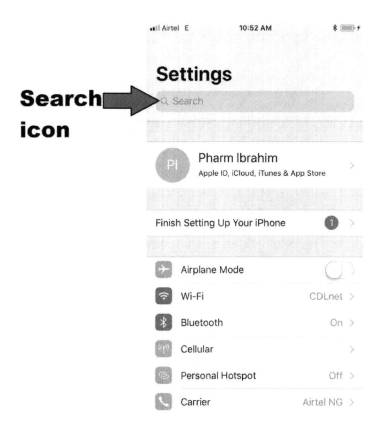

Search icon

Searching Your Device/Dictionary

You can search for information on your device or search for a word in dictionary.

To do this:

1. While on the Home screen, swipe down from the middle of the screen.

2. Tap the search field and type what you want to search for. The list filters as you type.

3. Tap a search result to open it.

Tip: To change what is included in the search results, go to **Settings**  > **Siri & Search**. Scroll down and tap an option (such as iBooks) and tap the status switch next to it.

Charging Your Device

If you are using your iPhone 8, iPhone 8 Plus or iPhone X more often (especially if you use Wi-Fi more often), you may realize that you need to charge your phone every day. One of the coolest times to charge your device is when you are taking a shower as you are not likely to be using it this time.

To learn more on how to use your phone for a longer time on battery, please go to page 214.

To charge your iPhone 8, iPhone 8 Plus, or iPhone X:

1. When you first open your product box, you will notice that the power cord consists of two parts (i.e. the **lightning to USB cable** and the **USB power adaptor**), connect these two parts together.

2. Connect the end of the **lightning to USB cable** to the lightning port of your device, making sure that both the

charging cable and the charging port on your device make a good contact.

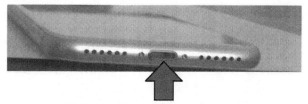

Lightning connector Port

3. Plug the power cord to an electrical outlet. The charging time may be long if you are using your device while charging it.

Tip: To customize battery options and increase the number of hours you use your phone; from the Home screen, tap on **Settings**, tap **Battery** and then select **Low Power Mode**. To see the percentage of battery remaining in the status bar, tap the indicator switch next to **Battery Percentage.**

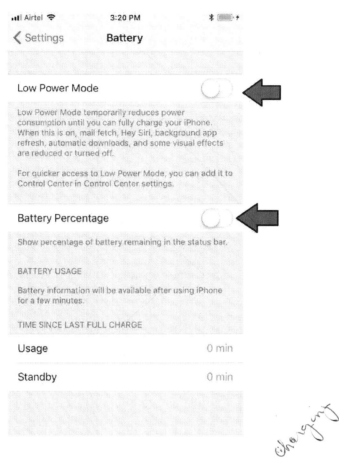

Note: *Please note that it is not advisable to use the lightning port while it is wet. If your phone has contact with water, please make sure you dry the lightning port before using it. Although your device is water resistant, it is not advisable at all to charge it while the device is wet. This may cause electric shock or damage your device.*

What About the Wireless Charging

iPhone 8, iPhone 8 Plus and iPhone X have a built-in wireless charging feature, and this means that you can charge the battery on your device using a wireless charger (sold separately).

To charge your device wirelessly:

- Using a USB cord, connect a power adapter to the wireless charger (sold separately) and then plug it to a wall socket. A wireless charger should come with a power adapter. iPhone 8, iPhone 8 Plus and iPhone X work with Qi chargers.

- If you are using your wireless charger for the first time, remove any protective nylon from the surface of the wireless charger. Then place your iPhone on the wireless charger following the instructions provided by the manufacturer of the wireless charger. Please note that if you connect a charger to your iPhone during wireless charging, the wireless charging feature may be unavailable.

In addition, depending on the type of the wireless charger you are using, charging wirelessly may take a longer time when compared to using a cable. This means that if you want to charge your device faster, you may consider using a cable.

What About the External Memory Card

As usual, the memories of iPhone 8, iPhone 8 Plus and iPhone X are not expandable.

Maintaining the Water and Dust Resistance

Although iPhone 8, iPhone 8 Plus and iPhone X are water and dust resistant, there are few things you still have to put at the back of your mind so that you don't spoil your phone. Some of those things you have to know are discussed below:

- iPhone 8, iPhone 8 Plus and iPhone X are water-resistant, but they are not waterproof. This means that you may be able to take a shower with your device without any problem, but probably wouldn't want to take it with you on a deep dive.
- Apple has made it known that it won't cover liquid/water damage on the iPhone 8/iPhone 8 Plus/iPhone X under the warranty so please be careful when using your phone under water.
- Splash, water, and dust resistance are not permanent conditions and resistance might decrease because of normal wear.
- The screen of your device may not respond properly when it is wet. I will advise that you clean it with a dry towel to get the full functionality.

- It is not advisable to put your device under water moving with force such as tap water . This is because water may get into the inner part of your device in the process. In addition, do not expose the device to salt water or ionized water.

- While your screen is wet, you may not enjoy using your device as you should. You may need to clean it with a dry towel to make it work properly.

- To avoid electric shock, please don't charge your device while it is wet or while it is under water.

Moving Your Items from Your Android Phone to Your iPhone 8, iPhone 8 Plus, or iPhone X

The easiest way to transfer your items from your old phone (Android Phone) to your new iPhone 8, iPhone 8 Plus, or iPhone X is through the use of **Move to iOS** app. To use this method, please follow the instructions below:

Please note that you can only use this method while setting up your new iOS device, if you have already set up your iPhone, this method may not work for you, unless you want to **erase your iPhone** (see page 217) and start over. Also, you will need internet connections on your Android phone and iPhone to use this method.

- Download **Move to iOS** app to your Android phone from Google store. Open the app and tap **Continue.** Accept the terms and tap **Next** at the top-right corner.

- While setting up your new iPhone, follow the onscreen prompts until you see **Apps & Data** screen. Tap **Move Data from Android,** and tap **Continue**. Then wait for a ten-digit or six-digit code to appear.
- On your Android device, enter the code. Then wait for the Transfer Data screen to appear. Select the content that you want to transfer and tap **Next.**
- When the transfer process is complete, tap **Done** on your Android device.
- On your iPhone, tap **Continue** and follow the onscreen steps to finish the setup process.

Using the Touch Screen

Your phone touch screen allows you to easily select items or perform functions. With the touch screen, you may operate your phone like a pro.

Notes:
- Do not tap/press the touch screen with sharp tools. Doing so may damage the touch screen or cause it to malfunction.
- Do not allow the touch screen to come into contact with other electrical appliances. This may cause the touch screen to malfunction.

- When the touch screen is wet, endeavor to clean it with a dry towel before using it. The touchscreen may not function properly when wet.
- For optimal use of the screen, you may need to remove screen protector before using it. However, good screen protector should be usable with your device.

You may control your touch screen with the following actions:

Tap: Touch once with your finger to select or launch a menu, application or option.

Tap and hold: Tap an item and hold it for more than a second to perform certain operations.

Tap and drag: Tap and drag with your finger, to move an item to a different location.

Pinch: Place two fingers far apart, and then draw them closer together to zoom out. Do the reverse to zoom in.

➢ **To Lock or Unlock the Touch Screen:**

When you do not use the device for a specified period, your device turns off the touch screen and automatically locks the touch screen so as to prevent any unwanted device operations and save battery. To adjust the automatic lock timing, go to **Settings** > **Display & Brightness** > **Auto-Lock**.

You can also manually lock the touch screen by pressing the side button.

To unlock, turn on the screen by pressing the side button and then drag the slider. If you have already set a lock screen password, you will be prompted to enter the password.

Note: You can change the lock screen method on your phone, please refer to page 52.

Rotating the Touch Screen

Your phone has a built-in motion sensor that detects its orientation. If you rotate your device, the interface will automatically rotate according to the orientation.

➢ **To activate or deactivate screen rotation**

Swipe up from the bottom edge of the screen to open Control Center, then tap ⬚. Please make sure you are swiping in from the bottom edge (lowest edge) of the screen to get what you want.

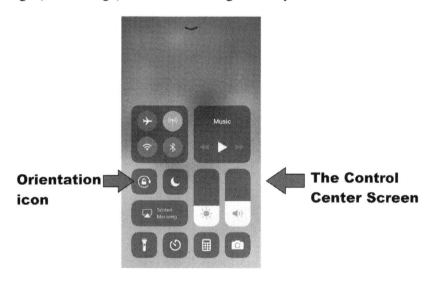

Orientation icon

The Control Center Screen

The Portrait orientation lock icon  should appear on the status bar when the screen orientation is locked.

Orientation icon on the status bar

Note: To access Action Center on iPhone X, swipe down from the top-right edge of the screen.

**Right-edge of the screen**

Overcoming the 'Back Button' Problem.

One feature you may quickly find missing if you are used to Android platform is dedicated back button. There is a way to solve this problem.

- Generally, when you are using an app you should find a small back icon (that looks like a triangle) at the top/lower left corner of the screen. Tap on this to go back to the previous page.

In-App Back Button

- Another way to go back to a previous page is to swipe from the left edge of the screen to right.

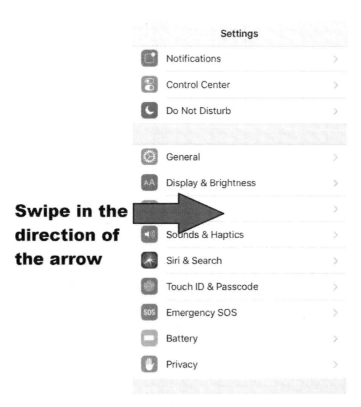

Swipe in the direction of the arrow

Tip: You may use this option to get out of any applicable page when you are done with the page and you don't see the done option.

Getting to Know the Home Screen

From your Home screen, you can view your phone status and access applications. Scroll left or right to see different apps/widgets on the Home screen.

Home Screen Layout:

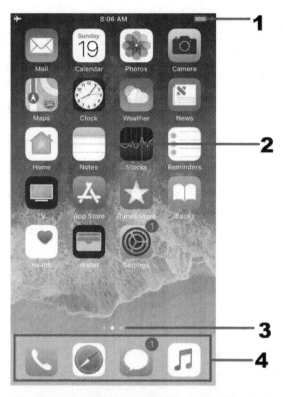

Number	Function
1.	**Status bar**: This is where status icons such as battery icon, Wi-Fi icon, etc. appear.
2.	**App shortcut icon:** Tap any of these icons to launch the corresponding app.
3.	**Home Screen Indicator:** This shows how many Home screens you have, and which one is currently visible.
4.	**iPhone Dock Icons:** These icons are your favorite icons. You can replace these icons with other ones. To learn how to do this, please see page 29.

Tip: You can select Home button's click force for your iPhone. To do this, go to **Settings** > **General** > **Home Button**, then choose a click force. You can choose among, 1, 2 and 3.

Note: If you are using iPhone 8 or 8 Plus, you can go to the Home Screen by pressing the Home button. To go to the Home Screen if you are using iPhone X, swipe up from the bottom edge of the screen.

Hint: If an app has a badge, you can clear this badge by following the method below.

- From the Home screen, tap Settings ⚙.
- Tap **Notifications.**
- Scroll to the app you want to clear its badge and tap it. In this case, I am trying to clear the badge on Message app.
- Tap the status switch next to **Badge App Icon**.

Please note that a badge is a notification number displayed on an app

icon, e.g.

Changing/Rearranging the Dock Icons

The dock icons are the four icons located at the bottom of the of the Home Screen. You can rearrange or change this icon to the one you like. To do this:

1. Long press an icon until the icons begin to shake or a small **X** icon appears and then lift your finger. You can long press any of the dock icons.

Note: You should press gently and lightly for the apps to shake. If you press firmly, you will get **3D Touch** (see page 167) options instead.

2. Then tap and drag the icon you want to move to another position.

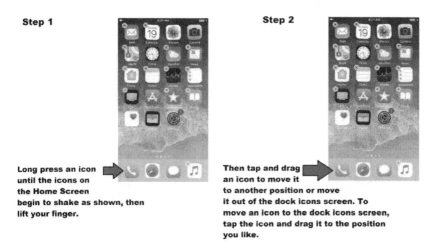

Step 1

Long press an icon until the icons on the Home Screen begin to shake as shown, then lift your finger.

Step 2

Then tap and drag an icon to move it to another position or move it out of the dock icons screen. To move an icon to the dock icons screen, tap the icon and drag it to the position you like.

Managing the Home Screen

To get more out of the Home screen, you will need to perform some tweaks.

- To move an app to another location on the Home screen, tap and hold an app until it starts to shake and then lift your finger. Then tap and drag the app to another location on the screen. Press the Home button to save your arrangement. To move an app to a different Home screen, drag the app to the edge of the screen.

Note: You should press gently and lightly for the apps to shake, if you press firmly, you will get **3D Touch** (see page 167) options instead.

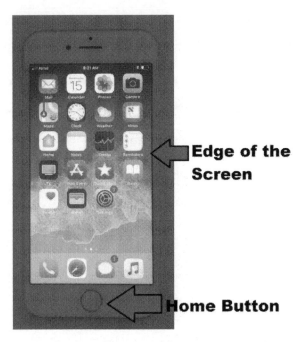

Edge of the Screen

Home Button

Note: To go to the Home Screen if you are using iPhone X, swipe up from the bottom edge of the screen.

- To remove an app from **iPhone dock** (the four bottom icons), tap and hold the icon until it begins to shake and then lift your finger. Then tap and drag it out of the dock and drop it at the main Home screen. Press the Home button to save your arrangement. To go to the Home Screen if you are using iPhone X, swipe up from the bottom edge of the screen. You can also drag any other app from the main Home screen to the iPhone dock to replace the removed app.

Note: You should press gently and lightly for the apps to shake. If you press firmly, you will get **3D Touch** (see page 167) options instead.

Tips:

- If you make a mistake and you wish to return your apps to the original arrangement, you can do so by following these steps. Go to **Settings** 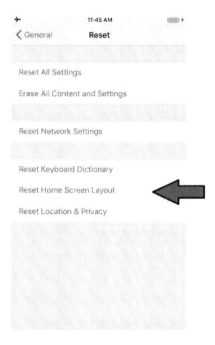 > **General** > **Reset**, then tap **Reset Home Screen Layout** to return the Home screen and apps to their original layout.

- To view widgets, swipe right from the left edge of the screen while on the Home screen.

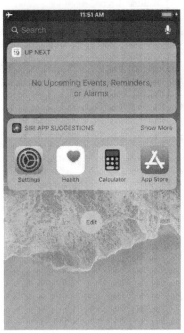

Widget Screen

To add more widgets, tap Edit and the tap the plus icon next to the widget you want to add. To remove a widget, tap the minus icon next to the widget you want to remove and then tap **Remove.**

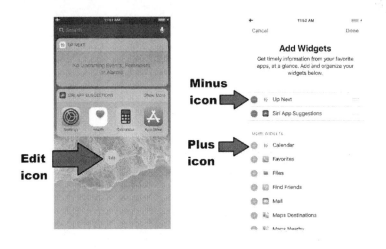

Managing the Home Screen Wallpaper

You can change the wallpaper settings for the Home screen and the locked screen.

1. While on the Home screen, tap on **Settings** ⊚ (To go to the Home screen from any screen, press the Home button. To go to the Home Screen if you are using iPhone X, swipe up from the bottom edge of the screen.)
2. Tap on **Wallpaper**.
3. Tap **Choose a New Wallpaper**.
4. Tap **Stills, Live** or **Dynamic**.

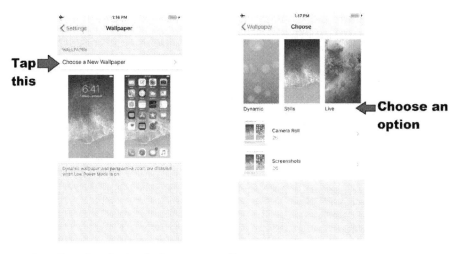

5. Tap the desired photo or wallpaper.
6. Tap **Still** or **Perspective** (located at the lower part of the screen). With Still selected, the wallpaper will always remain static. If Perspective is turned on, the wallpaper will move slightly when you move the phone.

7. Tap **Set** (located in the lower-right).

8. Tap an option:

    a. Set Lock Screen

    b. Set Home Screen

    c. Set Both

Note: When **Perspective** option is chosen, the wallpaper should shift slightly as you move the device.

To create a folder of items/apps:

1. From the Home screen, tap and hold an app until it starts to shake and then lift your finger. Then tap, drag and drop it onto another item/app to create a folder. Press the Home button when you finish. To go to the Home Screen if you are using iPhone X, swipe up from the bottom edge of the screen.)

   Note: You should press gently and lightly for the apps to shake. If you press firmly, you will get **3D Touch** (see page 167) options instead.

2. To rename a folder, tap the folder, and then tap and hold an app inside the folder. Thereafter, tap the **X** icon next to the name you want to change and enter a new name.

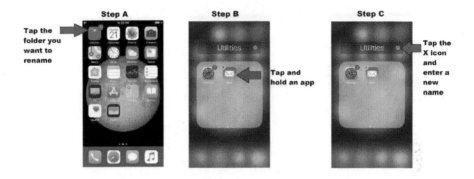

3. To add another app, from the Home screen, tap and hold an app, then drag and drop it onto a folder. Press the Home button when you finish. To go to the Home Screen if you are using iPhone X, swipe up from the bottom edge of the screen.)

4. To delete a folder, drag out all the apps. The folder will be deleted automatically after you remove all the apps inside it.

Accessing Applications

1. From the Home screen, tap on the app of your choice.

2. To go back to the app grid screen, press the Home button. To
   go to the Home Screen if you are using iPhone X, swipe up
   from the bottom edge of the screen.

Home Button

Accessing Recently Opened or Running Applications

1. Press the Home button twice quickly. A list of recently used apps appears on the screen. To access opened apps if you are using iPhone X, swipe up from the bottom of the screen and pause.

Swipe up and pause to access app switcher if you are using iPhone X

2. A preview window for each app will be displayed. Swipe the apps from left to right to view more apps.

3. To launch an app, tap on it.

4. To close an app, swipe up its preview window.

Uninstall an App

1. While on the Home screen, tap and hold the app you want to uninstall until it begins to shake.

   Note: You should press gently and lightly for the apps to shake. If you press firmly, you will get **3D Touch** (see page 167) options instead.

2. Tap the **X** next to the app you want to uninstall.

3. Tap **Delete** when prompted.

Understanding the Control Center

The Control Center provides a quick access to device functions such as Wi-Fi, allowing you to quickly turn them on or off.

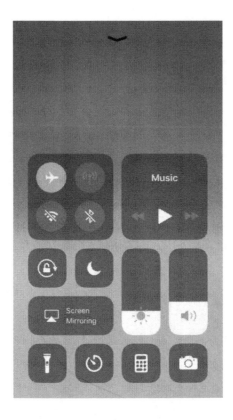

To view Control Center:

1. Swipe up from the bottom edge of the screen. You can also do this while on the lock screen. If you are using iPhone X, swipe down from the top-right edge of the screen.

2. Tap an icon to turn a feature on or off.

3. Swipe down from the top of the screen to dismiss Control Center. If you are using iPhone X, swipe up from bottom of the screen to close Control Center.

Tip: If there is a function/option that you will like to easily and quickly access, you can add it to Control Center. To add an option to the Control Center, go to **Settings** 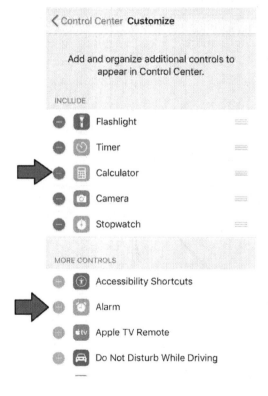 > **Control Center** > **Customize Controls**. Then tap the plus icon (+) next to the function/option you want to add. To remove an option, tap the red minus icon next to the option you want to remove.

Customizing Your Phone

You can get more done with your phone by customizing it to match your preferences.

To change your language:

1. From the Home screen, tap **Settings** .
2. Tap **General**.
3. Scroll down and tap **Language & Region**.

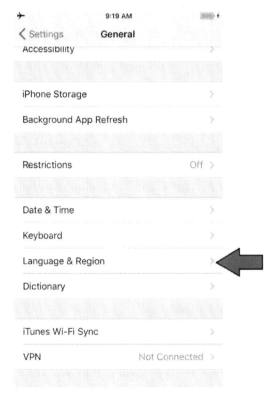

4. Tap **iPhone Language** and then select a language from the list.

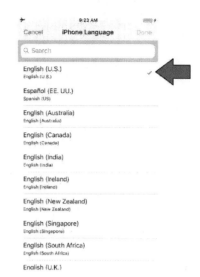

5. Tap **Done** located at the top of the screen.

Set the current time and date

Your device is built to update its time automatically, but you may need to manually set your time for one reason or the other. To manually set time and date:

1. From the Home screen, tap **Settings** .
2. Tap **General**.
3. Scroll down and tap **Date & Time.**
4. To ensure that the time on your device is updated automatically, move the switch next to **Set Automatically** to on.

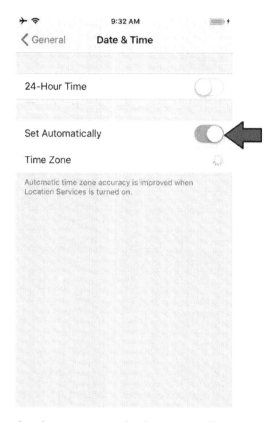

5. To set the time on your device manually or prevent your device from updating the time automatically, move the switch next to **Set Automatically** to off, and then edit the time and date as you desire.

6. To manage the time zone settings, move the switch next to **Set Automatically** to off, and then tap **Time Zone.**

7. To use a 24-hour time setting for your device, move the switch next to **24-Hour Time** to on.

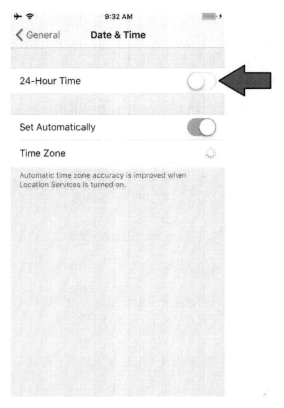

To control sounds and vibrations:

1. From the Home screen, tap **Settings** .
2. Scroll down and tap **Sounds & Haptics**.
3. Tap an option.

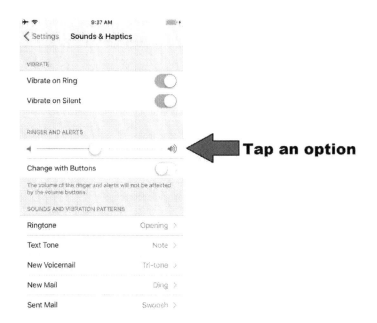

Tap an option

4. To control the volume of ringer and alerts, draw the small circle on the volume slider.

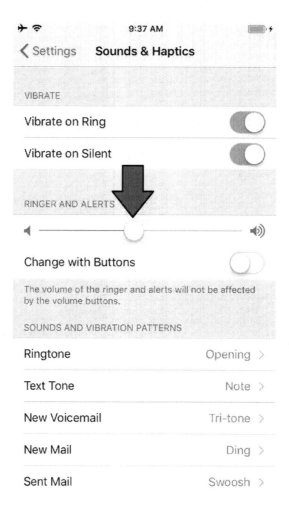

5. If you don't want an alert to give a sound, for example, if you don't want to receive sound when you get calendar alerts, tap **Calendar Alerts** and then tap **None.**

To adjust the phone volume:

Press the **Volume key** up or down, this key is located at the left side of your phone (when the phone is facing you).

Setting a Home screen, lock screen or Home and lock screen image

You can set a Home screen, lock screen or Home and lock screen image to the one of your choice. To do this please refers to page 34.

Adjusting the brightness of the display

1. Swipe up from the bottom edge of the screen. If you are using iPhone X, swipe down from the top-right edge of the screen. Then drag the slider as you like to adjust the brightness.

Drag this bar up or down to adjust the brightness.

Hint: The brightness level of the display will affect how quickly your device consumes battery power. I will advise that you turn it reasonably low if you are very concerned about saving energy. In addition, when auto-brightness/True Tone is turned on, the brightness will adjust automatically depending on the lighting conditions. To disable this feature, go to **Settings** > **Display & Brightness.** Then tap the switch next to **True Tone**.

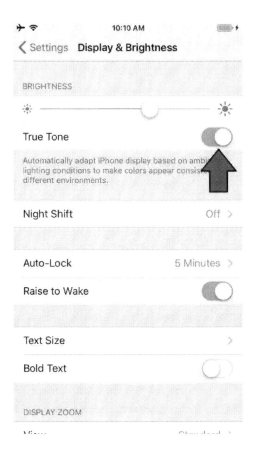

To set a lock screen:

You can lock your phone by activating the lock screen feature.

Note: Once you set a screen lock, your phone will require an unlock code each time you turn it on or unlock the touch screen.

1. From the Home screen, tap **Settings** .
2. Scroll down and tap **Touch ID & Security**.
3. Tap **Turn Passcode On**.

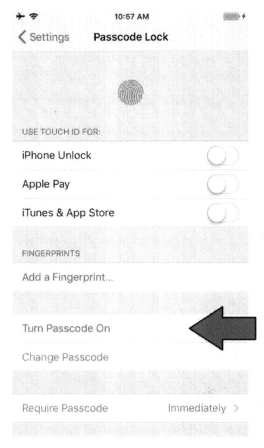

USE TOUCH ID FOR:

iPhone Unlock

Apple Pay

iTunes & App Store

FINGERPRINTS

Add a Fingerprint...

Turn Passcode On

Change Passcode

Require Passcode   Immediately ›

4. Enter a 6-digit passcode. Re-enter your passcode.

5. To turn off passcode, tap **Turn Passcode Off**.

6. In addition, you may choose **Add a Fingerprint.**

Tip: You can tell your device to wake up whenever you pick it up

from a surface. To do this, from the Home screen, tap **Settings**
> **Display & Brightness > Raise to Wake** and tap the status switch
to activate this option. Please note that this option may consume
your battery faster when enabled.

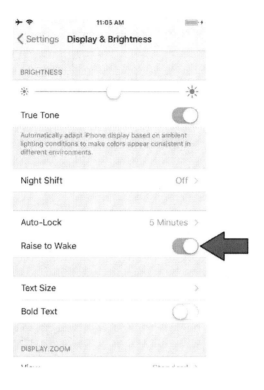

Your iPhone Name

The name of your iPhone is used by iTunes and iCloud.

To change the name of your iPhone:

1. From the Home screen, tap **Settings** .
2. Tap **General**.
3. Tap **About**.
4. Tap **Name** and enter a new name.

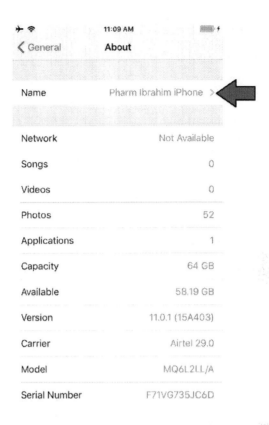

Entering a Text

You can enter a text by selecting characters on the virtual keypad or by speaking words into the microphone through use of voice command.

Note: You can change the writing language to any one supported. For more information, please see below.

To enter a text:

1. Enter a text by selecting the corresponding alphabets or numbers.

2. You can use any of the following keys:

Please note that the on-screen keyboard on your phone may be different from the one shown below. This is because the on-screen keyboard you see depends on the text input field you selected. The one shown below is the one you should see when you want to compose a text message.

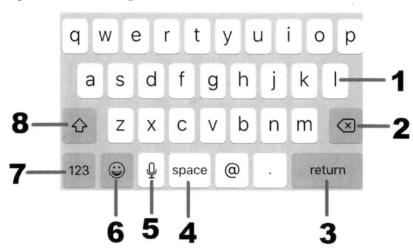

Number	Function
1.	Virtual Alphabet. To type an alternate character, tap and hold an alphabet and then slide your finger to choose an option.
2.	Clear your input/backspace.
3.	Start a new line. It also acts as **Go/Done** button.
4.	Space bar: Use this button to insert space between words.
5.	**Voice input/typing button**.
6.	**Emoticons button.** To go back to ABC functions after pressing the emoticons key, tap **ABC**. When you press and hold this key, you will access more

	functions like Keyboard settings and One-Handed keyboard.
7.	Switch between Number and ABC mode.
8.	Change case. To permanent upper case, double tap this button.

Hints:

Your keyboard suggests words as you type, you can tap on any suggestion to choose it.

If you tap a wrong key, you can slide your finger to the correct key. Interestingly, the letter isn't entered until you release your finger from a key.

If you have more than one keyboard language installed, tap to switch between them.

To add input languages:

1. From the Home screen, tap **Settings** 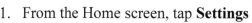.
2. Tap **General**.
3. Tap **Keyboard**.
4. Tap **Keyboards** to view a list of saved keyboards.
5. Tap **Add New Keyboard.** Tap the keyboard you wish to add.

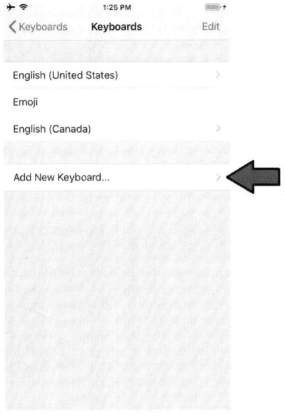

When you select two or more languages, you can switch between the

input languages by tapping on .

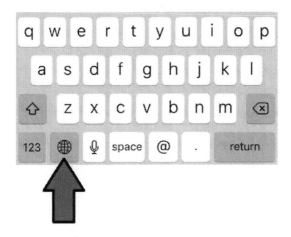

Please note that the icon shown above may not appear on your keyboard if you have not added more than one language to the keyboard.

Tip: You can customize your virtual keyboard the way you like. To do this:

1. From the Home screen, tap **Settings** .
2. Tap **General**.
3. Tap **Keyboard** and tap an option.

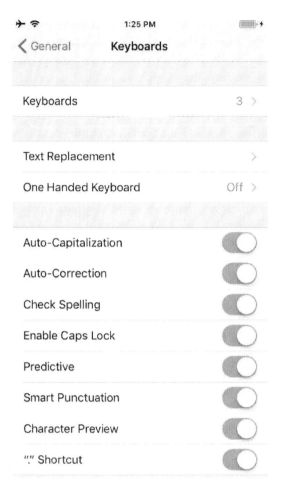

To copy and paste a text:

While you are entering a text, you can use the copy and paste feature to use the text in other applications.

1. Double-tap or tap and hold a word, and then drag ◦ or ◦ to select the text you want.

Tap this icon to access more options

Drag either of these two icons to select the texts you want

2. Select the **Copy** option to copy, or select the **Cut** option to cut the text onto the clipboard.

3. In another application or where you want to place the text, double-tap the text input field.

4. Select the **Paste** option to insert the text from the clipboard into the text input field.

Using The Special Features

iPhone 8, iPhone 8 Plus and iPhone X come with special features that differentiate them from other smartphones. I will now explain how to use these features.

Using the Touch ID

One of the cool features on iPhone 8 and iPhone 8 Plus is the Touch ID/Fingerprint scanner. It allows you to unlock applications without entering boring passwords. Please note that iPhone X does not have a Touch ID.

Registering Your Fingerprint

Before you can begin to use the Touch ID, you will need to first register your fingerprint. You have the chance of registering more than one fingerprints. To do this:

1. From the Home screen, tap **Settings** .
2. Tap **Touch ID & Passcode**.
3. If you have setup a passcode, you will need to enter it. If you have not, you may need to setup one.
4. Tap **Add a Fingerprint**.

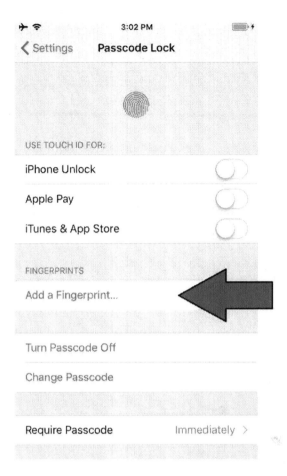

5. Place your finger on the Home button. Then repeatedly lift and gently press your finger against the Home button.

6. Tap **Continue**.

7. Lift and rest the edge of your finger on the Home button repeatedly. Then tap **Continue.**

8. If you have not done so before you may need to enter a backup passcode.

9. If you would like to use the Touch ID to unlock your phone, tap the status switch beside **iPhone Unlock** to enable it.

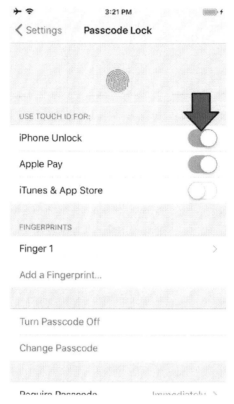

10. If you would like to use the Touch ID with Apple Pay, tap the status switch next to **Apple Pay**.

11. To unlock your phone when your phone locks, press the Home Key with one of the fingers whose print has been saved.

Renaming Fingerprints

1. From the Home screen, tap **Settings** .

2. Tap **Touch ID & Passcode.**

3. If you have setup a passcode, you will need to enter it.

4. Tap the fingerprint you want to rename.

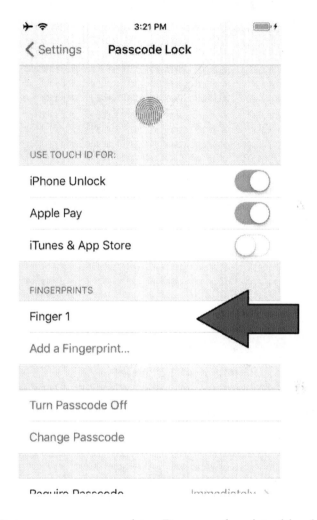

5. Enter a new name and tap **Done** on the virtual keyboard.

Deleting Fingerprints

1. From the Home screen, tap **Settings** .
2. Tap **Touch ID & Passcode**.

3. If you have setup a passcode, you will need to enter it.

4. Tap the fingerprint you want to delete.

5. Tap **Delete Fingerprint**.

Troubleshooting the Touch ID/Fingerprint Scanner

If the Touch ID is not responding, try any of the following:

1. Remove any screen protector that may be covering the fingerprint scanner located on the Home button.

2. Ensure that you are not using the tip of your fingerprint. Make sure to cover the entire Home key with your finger.

3. If your finger has scars, try registering another finger, this is because your device may not recognize fingerprints that are affected by wrinkles or scars.

4. Make sure you use the finger you used to register your fingerprint.

5. Make sure that your finger and the surface of the fingerprint scanner are clean and dry.

Using the Face ID

The Face ID allows you to unlock your phone by looking at it. Please note that this feature is only available on iPhone X.

Registering Your Face ID

Before you can begin to use the Face ID, you will need to first register it. To do this:

1. From the Home screen, tap **Settings** .
2. Tap **Face ID & Passcode**.
3. If you have setup a passcode, you will need to enter it.
4. Tap Set up Face ID, and follow the prompts.

Water Resistance

Another feature that makes iPhone 8, iPhone 8 Plus and iPhone X unique is the water resistivity. You don't have to worry that your phone is going to get wet when you are inside the rain. To know more about water resistivity, please go to page 18.

The Siri

Siri is a trained virtual assistant that has been built to answer questions, and interestingly, you probably don't need any technical training to use this feature. If you need any, it will be some tweaks and how to ask questions. That is what this section of the guide is mainly for. This section of the guide will show you how to manage Siri like a maven and how to ask questions and give commands that Siri will understand.

Getting Started with Siri

You should have the option to set up Siri when you first start using your phone. If you skip this step during the phone setup and you will like to do it now, then go to the phone settings 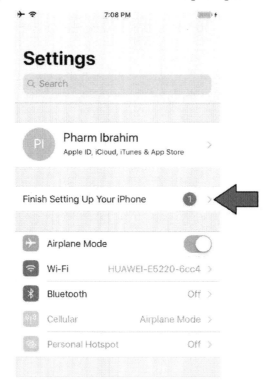 and tap **Finish Setting Up Your iPhone** and follow the prompts.

1. You can get the attention of Siri in several ways:

    • Press and hold the Home button, release the button, then make your request. If you are using iPhone X, press the side button until Siri function appears.

- Press and hold the Home button, make your request and then release the Home button when you are done speaking.

  Please note that you may need to enable this option to use this method, to do this go to **Settings** > **Siri & Search** > **Press Home for Siri**.

- Say **Hey Siri** and then make your request. Please note that you may need to enable this feature. To do this, **Settings** > **Siri & Search** > then tap the switch next to **Listen for "Hey Siri"**.

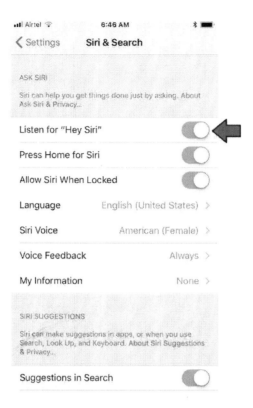

2. An audio wave moves across your screen, letting you know Siri is listening and processing your request.

3. To give another command to Siri, tap the **continue to listen** button (located at the bottom of the screen) or say **Hey Siri** followed by the command.

Note: You may notice that the question you asked Siri is different from what it types on the screen (what Siri types on the screen is what it thought you have said), I will advise that you always try to speak clearly.

Understanding the Siri's Interface

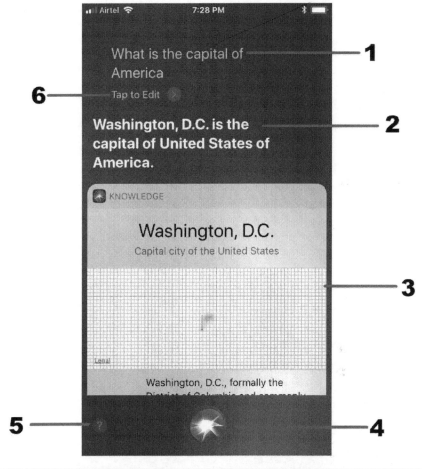

Number	Function
1.	Your Question
2.	Siri's Response
3.	More info tab. You can scroll down this tab to access more information or access more info link.
4.	Tap this icon to continue speaking to Siri.

5.	Tap on this to access the help page.
6.	Tap this to edit a misinformation using the onscreen keyboard.

Getting What You Want from Siri

There are many things you can ask Siri to do for you and before you finish reading this guide you will learn how to effectively interact with it.

I will like to mention that interacting with Siri is not an examination (so there is nothing like cheating) and you can get help by tapping on

the question mark icon  on the Siri menu. You can also ask Siri **"What can you do?"**.

Allowing Siri to Access Your Apps

You can choose which app you want Siri to support:

1. From the Home screen, tap **Settings**  .
2. Tap **Siri & Search**.
3. Scroll down, tap an app, and then tap the status switch next to **Search & Siri Suggestions**.

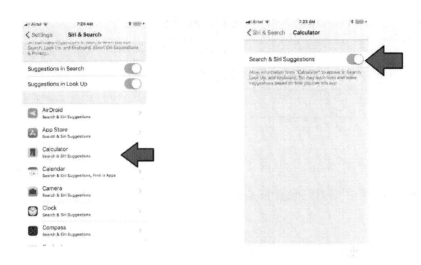

Using Siri to Open Apps or Programs

One of those things you will want to use Siri to do is accessing your apps. You can quickly open an app by saying **Open** and then mentioning the name of the app. For example, to open Settings, say **Open settings.** To open calculator, say **Open calculator**.

You may also say **Launch settings** instead of **Open settings.**

In addition, you may give a more specific command like **Open sound settings** to go to sound settings. Say **Launch Wi-Fi Settings** to open the Wi-Fi settings.

Using Siri with Calendar

One of the fantastic features that Siri can do for you is making an appointment. This virtual assistant is fully integrated with your device Calendar making it easy for it to make appointments for you.

With just few commands you can get Siri to put an event or appointment into your calendar. To do this:

1. Press and hold the Home button, then release the button. If you are using iPhone X, press the side button until Siri function appears.

2. Alternatively, you can get Siri's attention by saying **Hey Siri**.

3. Then say whatever you want to include in the Calendar. For example, you can say the following:

   • Create an appointment with Clinton for Monday at 1 p.m.

   • Schedule a conference with John at 10 a.m. on Sunday.

   • Remind me to fix my car at 5 p.m. today. Please note that you can also say all the examples given above in other ways, the most important thing is to get Siri to understand what you are saying.

   • When it has gotten the information, the Calendar will appear on the Siri menu. You can then tap or say

Confirm/Yes if you are satisfied with the response. If not, tap or say **Cancel.**

You can also make changes to your Calendar using Siri. To do this:

1. Repeat the first step above.

2. Then say what you want it to change. For example, you may say any of the following:

   - Change the appointment scheduled with Clinton on Monday at 1 p.m. to 3 p.m.

   - Cancel my appointment scheduled for 9 a.m. on Sunday.

In addition, you can check how your Calendar looks like today. To do this

Tap the **continue to listen** icon and say, "**How does my calendar look like today?**" Or say, "**Do I have any appointment today**?" Or just any variant. Note that you can also ask Siri about your Calendar for a day in the future. To do this, say "**Do I have any appointment scheduled for tomorrow**".

Using Siri to Setup Reminders

There are probably many things going through your mind and it will be quite interesting if you can get a personal assistant to assist in remembering some of your duties. Interestingly, Siri can help you in this regard.

To set a reminder using Siri:

1. Press and hold the Home button, then release the button. If you are using iPhone X, press the side button until Siri function appears.

2. Alternatively, you can get Siri's attention by saying **Hey Siri**.

3. Then say whatever you want to include in the Reminder. For example, you can say the following:

   - Remind me to fix the car by 3 p.m.

   - Remind me to drop the cake at the restaurant.

   - Remind me to pick my daughter by 4 p.m.

   - Remind me to call Ibrahim at 1 p.m.

4. When it has gotten the information, the reminder will appear. You can then confirm or cancel the reminder.

Please note that it is not compulsory that you put remind in every statement as I did above, but I will advise that you do this whenever you can. This is because it will help Siri to easily get what you are saying and avoid any confusion.

Using Siri with Alarm

You can also set an alarm using this personal assistant. To do this:

1. Press and hold the Home button, then release the button. If you are using iPhone X, press the side button until Siri function appears.

2. Alternatively, you can get Siri's attention by saying **Hey Siri**.

3. Say the time for alarm. For example, you can say: "**set an alarm for 1 p.m. tomorrow**" or "**alarm for 1 p. m tomorrow**". Please note that Siri may be unable to set an alarm for more than one day (around 24 hours) ahead.

4. When it has gotten the information, the alarm will appear, and it will tell you that it has set the alarm.

Using Siri with Clock

You can ask Siri what your local time is. In addition, it can also tell you the time in a specific place.

1. Press and hold the Home button, then release the button. If you are using iPhone X, press the side button until Siri function appears.

2. Alternatively, you can get Siri's attention by saying **Hey Siri**.

3. Then say, "**What is the time?**" or say, "**What is the time in New York?**"

Using Siri to Get Flight Information

You can also use this virtual assistant to get information about a flight. This is a smarter way to know when an airplane will take off.

For example, you can say **"What is the flight status of Delta 400?"** to get the flight information about this flight.

Using Siri with Weather App

To know about the weather, just say **"What's the weather going to be today?"**. You may also know about the weather condition of a place by asking **"What is the weather of New York today?"**.

Using Siri with Mail App/ Message App

You can instruct Siri to compose an email/message for you. To do this:

1. Press and hold the Home button, then release the button. If you are using iPhone X, press the side button until Siri function appears.

2. Alternatively, you can get Siri's attention by saying **Hey Siri**.

3. Then say the subject and the person you want to email. For example, you can say:

   - Send an email to Ibrahim about the meeting.

   - Send an SMS to Clinton

Please note that you may need to enable some apps before Siri can communicate with them. Please refers to page 72 to learn more.

In addition, note that you will usually have to include one or more information before you can send the email. For example, you may need to say the body of the email before you send it.

Using Siri with Map App

You can also use the Siri to search the map. This virtual assistant is fully integrated with the Map app on your device. To get how the map of a place looks like:

1. Repeat the first step above.

2. Then say the map of an area you want to get. For example, you may say:

    - Show me the New York map.

    - Show me the map of Seattle.

    - Give me the directions to John F. Kennedy International Airport.

What about Math?

Siri can also help you with some mathematics and conversions. For example, you can tell Siri **"What is the square root of four?"**. You may also say **"convert one foot to centimeter"** or **"What is the exchange rate between dollars and pounds?"** and so on. As I have said before, the most important thing is to make sure Siri gets the message you are trying to get across.

Using Siri to Get Definitions of Words

You can quickly check for the meaning of a word by asking Siri. For example, you may say **"What is the meaning of flabbergasted?"**.

Siri's Options

The tab under Siri allows you to manage Siri's functions. To access these options:

1. From the Home screen, tap **Settings** 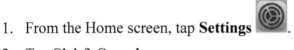.
2. Tap **Siri & Search**.

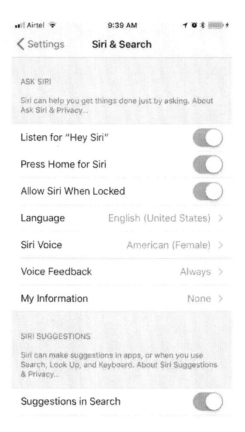

The options may include:

Listen for "Hey Siri": If this option is enabled, you will be able to get the attention of Siri by saying **Hey Siri**.

Allow Siri When Locked: This option allows you to access to Siri from the lock screen.

Language: Allows you to customize language settings of Siri.

Siri Voice: Use this option to select Siri Voice.

Voice Feedback: Tap this option to customize feedback settings.

My Information: Tap this for your information.

Troubleshooting Siri

Although much efforts have been put into making this virtual assistant, I am quite sure that Siri will misbehave at one time or the other. When this happens, there are few things to do.

- **Ensure that you are connected to a strong network**: If you have a bad or no internet connection, Siri may not work properly. Therefore, the first thing to check when Siri starts to misbehave is the internet connection.

- **Speak clearly in a silent place**: Make sure you are speaking clearly and try to avoid background noise.

- **Tap the continue listen button**: Tap the continue listen button , if the device does not hear you, or to give it another command.

- **Try to restart your smartphone**: If you find out that all what I have mentioned above does not work, you may try restarting your device because it may be that it is your device that is confused and not Siri.

Using the Web

Safari App

Opening the Safari

1. From the Home screen, tap **Safari** icon.

Get to Know the Safari's Interface

The screenshot below will introduce you to various buttons found on Safari:

Islam Question and Answer — 2

General Supervisor: Shaykh Muhammad Saalih al-Munajjid

Thu 5 Rb1 1439 - 23 November 2017

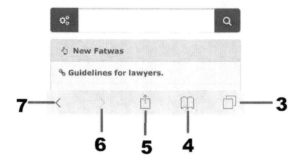

7 ← → ↑ ⌂ ⧉ — 3

6 5 4

1	Refresh**: Tapping this icon reloads a webpage.**
2	**Webpage view**: Webpage information is shown here. To zoom, place your two fingers on the screen and spread them apart or do the reverse.
3	**Tabs:** Tap this to navigate between different webpages. To close an app, tap the tab icon and then tap the **X** icon next to the thumbnail of the page you want to close.
4	**Bookmark:** Tap this icon to access bookmark pages, reading list and history.
5	**Menu icon:** Tap this icon to access more options such as **Find on Page, Create PDF, Print** etc.
6	**Forward**: Tap this icon to return to the page you just left.
7	**Back:** Tap this icon to revisit the page you just visited.
8	**Address bar**: Tapping this bar let you enter the web address of a page. You may also type in search phrase into the address bar.

Hint: If you mistakenly tap a wrong button, don't panic, just keep holding your finger on the wrong button and then stylishly move away your finger (just as if you are dragging the wrong icon) to stop the command from executing. Generally, commands don't get executed until you release you finger.

Using the Address/Search Bar

Every web browser must have an address bar and Safari also has one. This bar serves the function of URL address bar and search bar. You can change the default search engine used by Safari. To learn how to change the search engine to another one, please go to page 95.

You choose whether to launch a webpage or search for a term based on what you type into the address bar. For example, if you type **Windows Radar** into the address bar and tap **Go**, Google/Bing search results for that phrase is displayed. On the other hand, if you type **windowsradar.com** and tap **Go**, you will be taken to the website bearing the name.

When you begin to type inside the address bar, Safari automatically makes suggestions beneath your typing. You can choose one of these suggestions to make things faster.

If you don't want to see suggested search terms, go to **Settings** > **Safari**, then turn off **Search Engine Suggestions** and **Safari Suggestions**.

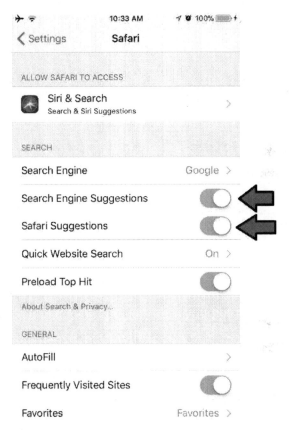

Zooming a Webpage in Safari

To zoom in a webpage in Safari, place two fingers on the webpage and spread them apart. To zoom out, place two fingers on the webpage and move them closer together.

Using Tabs on Safari

The tabs allow you to open different webpages at once. You can open many tabs at once on Safari. Please see the screenshot under **Get to know the Safari's Interface** to have a pictorial view of the Safari tab icon.

To manage the browsing tabs:

1. Tap the tab icon .
2. To open a new tab, tap + icon.

3. To open a tab, tap the desired tab.

4. To close a tab, tap the **X** icon at the top left corner of the thumbnail of the tab you want to close. See the picture above.

Favorites (Bookmarks)

With several billions of webpages in the internet world, you just
have to select your favorites. Just like other modern-day browsers,
Safari gives you the opportunity to select a favorite or bookmark a
page. This makes it easier to visit the website or webpage in the
future.

To bookmark a webpage:

1. Open the website you want to bookmark.

2. Tap **Menu icon** (located at the bottom of the screen).
    You may see the screenshot under **Get to know the Safari's
    Interface** to have a pictorial view of the menu icon.

3. Tap **Add Bookmark** or **Add to Favorites**.

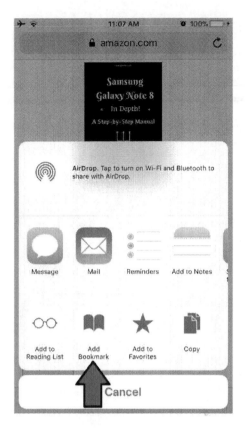

4. Key in the appropriate name for the bookmark or favorite.

5. Tap **Save**.

Accessing Your Bookmarks/Favorites

After you have added a webpage to your favorites list, you will need to access this list sooner or later. To access your bookmarks, tap the

Bookmarks ▭ (located at the bottom of the screen) and then tap **Favorites**.

Save a Reading List for Later

Webpages contain a lot of information and you will probably need to schedule some webpages for later reading. Saving a webpage in the reading list is a great way to do this. When you find an interesting information online and you don't have the time to read it now, you can save it for a later reading.

To save a reading list for later, open the webpage and tap located at the bottom or top of the screen, then tap **Add to Reading List**.

Accessing Your Reading List

After you have saved a page in the reading list, you will need to access this list sooner or later. To do this, tap the Bookmarks (located at the bottom of the screen) and then tap .

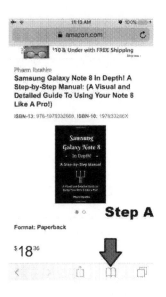

Step A

Step B

Changing the Search Engine

You may not love the default search engine on Safari and you may want to change it to another one.

You can change the Safari Search Engine by following the steps highlighted below:

1. From the Home screen, tap **Settings** .
2. Tap **Safari**.
3. Tap on **Search Engine** and select a search engine. Then tap the back button located at the top left corner of the screen.

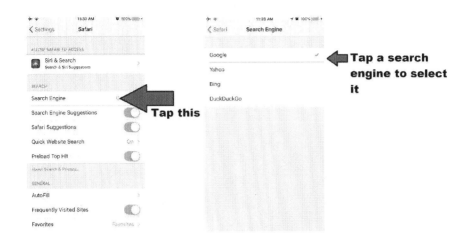

Managing the History List

If the private mode is not enabled, Safari collects the history of the webpages you visit and stores it.

To access your history:

1. Tap the Bookmarks 📖 (located at the bottom of the screen).

2. Tap **History** 🕐.

Hint: To clear browsing data, repeat the two steps above and tap **Clear.** Then select whether you are clearing the browsing data of **The last hour, Today, Today and yesterday, and All time**. To cancel this process, tap **Cancel**.

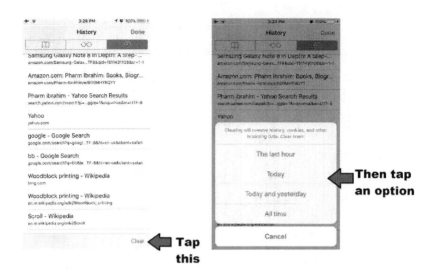

Sharing a Webpage with Friends

To share your webpage with friends, open the Safari app and tap

. Then choose a social media from the sharing options that
appears.

Private Browsing

There are times when you will not want your browser to save any
information about your visit to a webpage. For instance, if you don't
want a website to save cookies on your device or you don't want
your child to know you are browsing about favorite gifts to buy for
them.

In addition, Private mode browsing allows for multiple sessions. For example, you may access your Yahoo mail account (or another web account) on a normal window and use the Private mode tab to open the Yahoo mail account of that of your friend or family member without logging out of your own account. Pages viewed in Private mode are not listed in your browser history or search history, and leave no traces (such as cookies) on your device.

To activate the Private browsing, tap the tab ⬜ icon and tap **Private.** Then tap the plus icon (+) to open a webpage in private mode.

To exit the Private mode, tap the tab ⬛ icon and then tap the **X** next to the thumbnail of the site you want to close.

Please note that you have to close the webpage opened in private mode to prevent Safari from opening the last webpage you visited when you access the private mode.

To go back to normal browsing, tap the tab button ⬛ and then tap **Private**.

Add Your Favorite Webpage to the Home Screen

You can make your favorite webpage a shortcut on the Home screen. This allows you to easily access the webpage directly from your Home screen. To do this:

1. Open the webpage and tap on .

2. Scroll to the left and tap **Add to Home Screen**.

Using Distraction-free Reading

Distraction-free reading removes adverts and other distracting items from a webpage. To use this feature, open the webpage and tap on ☰ next to the address bar. To exit the distraction-free reading, tap this icon again.

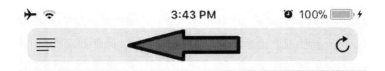

Please note that this feature may not be available on all webpages.

More on the More Options Tab

Many options under the more options tab have already been discussed, but I will still like to point out few more things.

1. **Print:** Use this option to print a webpage. To print a webpage, simply tap **Print** and follow the prompts.

2. **Find on Page:** Use this option to search for a word or a phrase on a webpage.

3. **Request desktop site:** Use this option to request the desktop version of a webpage.

4. **Create PDF:** Tap this to save a webpage as a PDF. To do this, simply tap **Create PDF,** and tap **Done** located at the top of the screen. Then tap **Save File To…,** choose a location and tap **Done** located at the top of the screen.

Tip: To access more options while on the more option screen, swipe left or right.

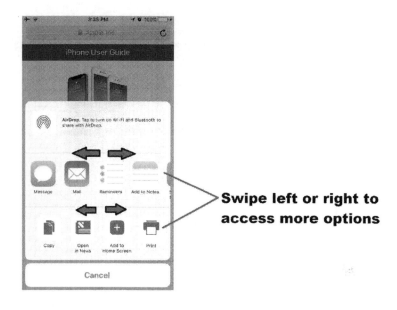

Swipe left or right to access more options

Troubleshooting Internet Connection when Using Safari

Safari may sometimes refuse to browse the internet. When this happens, you may try any of the suggestions below:

1. Check if you are connected to a Wireless network. If your phone is not connected to a network, from a Home screen, tap **Settings** > **Wi-Fi**. Then tap the status switch to turn Wi-Fi on. When the wireless network is active, you should see this icon 📶 on the status bar at the top of the screen.

2. If you are trying to use a cellular connection and not a Wi-Fi connection, then check your cellular data connection. From

the Home screen, tap **Settings** 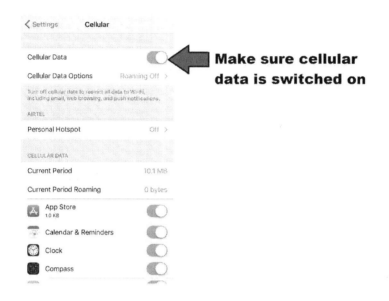 > **Cellular** > **Cellular Data**.

Make sure cellular data is switched on

3. If you are trying to roam while abroad, check that you have allowed roaming. From the Home screen, tap **Settings** > **Cellular** > **Cellular Data Options**. Then ensure **Data Roaming** is enabled. Please note that when roaming, international roaming charges may apply.

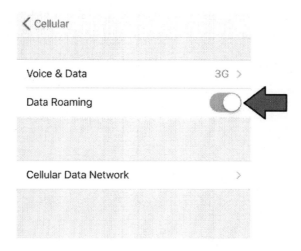

You may contact your network service provider if your phone still refuses to browse after trying all what I have mentioned above.

Communication

Calling

Learn how to use the calling functions, such as making and answering calls, using options available during a call and using call-related features.

Depending on your network service provider, please note that the descriptions in this section of the guide may be different from the one on your device.

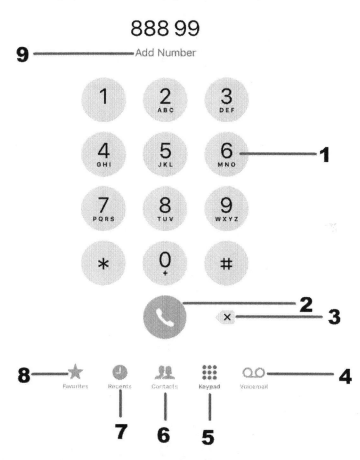

Number	Function
1.	Keypad numbers.
2.	**Call button**: Tap this to make a call.
3.	**Delete/Backspace**.
4.	**Voicemail button:** Tap this to check your voicemail or setup voicemail.
5.	**Keypad button:** Tap this to hide or show the keypad.

6.	**Contacts:** Access your contacts.
7.	**Recents**: Tap this to access call log. To access more information about a call, tap (i).
8.	**Favorites:** Tap this to access your favorite list.
9.	**Add number:** Use this option to add a number to your contacts.

To Make a Call or Silence a Call

1. While on the Home screen, tap **Phone** and enter a phone number. If the keypad does not appear on the screen, tap the keypad button Keypad to show the keypad. To call a number on your contact, tap the **Contact** button on the Phone app screen.

2. Tap to make a call.

3. To silence an incoming call, press the volume down button.

Hint: You can access apps/items on your phone while receiving a call. Press the Home key located at the lower side of the screen (to go to the Home Screen if you are using iPhone X, swipe up from the bottom edge of the screen) and tap on the item/app. To return to the call, tap the green bar at the top of the screen.

In addition, you can use Siri to call or send a message, open the Siri app, and say **Call** or **Text** and then the contact's name.

Note: If your phone is not ringing aloud, check if you have not mistakenly enabled the silent mode. To turn on/off the silent mode, flip the ring/silent button located at the side of the phone (the button located next to volume buttons).

To Answer a Call or Reject an Incoming Call:

1. To receive an incoming call, tap **Accept (the green phone icon).**
2. To decline an incoming call, tap **Decline (the red phone icon)**.
3. To reply with a text, tap **Message** and then tap one of the pre-written messages or tap **Custom...,** and write your message.
4. To remind yourself to return the call, tap **Remind Me**, then indicate when you want to be reminded.

Notes: If you are using an app, a pop-up screen is displayed for the incoming call, just tap the corresponding icon to accept or decline the call.

In addition, you can create rejection messages of your own. From the Home screen, tap **Settings** > **Phone** > **Respond with Text**, then tap any of the default messages to edit it.

Learn How to Use Your Phone During a Call

You can perform any of these tasks when on a call:

Depending on your network service provider, please note that the screenshot shown below may be different from the one on your device.

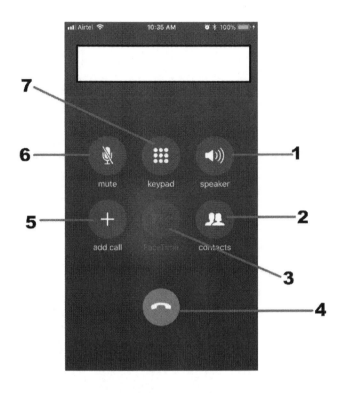

Number	Function
1.	To turn Speakerphone on or off, tap this icon.
2.	Tap contacts to view stored contacts.
3.	Tap FaceTime to initiate a video call with another iOS or Mac OS user.
4.	Tap this icon to **end a call**.
5.	Tap add call icon to begin conference calling.
6.	Mute the microphone.
7.	Tap this icon to access the keypad.

Tip: To access the application screen while on call, press the Home button. To return to the call, tap the green bar at the top of the screen. To go to the Home Screen if you are using iPhone X, swipe up from the bottom edge of the screen.

Place a New Call While on a Call (Conference Calling)

If your network service provider supports this feature, you can make another call while a call is in progress.

1. From the active call screen, tap + **Add call**.
2. Choose a contact and tap the call icon.
3. To add a number that isn't in your contacts, tap Keypad

    located at the bottom of the screen. Enter the number

   and then tap the Call icon.
4. When the call is answered:

   i.   Tap **Swap** to switch between the two calls.

   ii.   Tap **Merge calls** to turn the call to a conference call.
5. To end a call while in the Conference call mode, tap the **info**

   ⓘ icon (next to **Conference call**) and then **End**.
6. To talk privately with one person in a conference call, tap the

   Info ⓘ button, then tap **Private** next to the person. Tap Merge Calls to resume the conference call.

7. To end all calls, tap the red key.

Emergency Calling

You can use iPhone 8, iPhone 8 Plus or iPhone X to make an

emergency call. From the Home screen, tap **Phone** icon and
enter the emergency telephone number. Note that if you dial 911 in
the U.S, your location details may be provided to emergency service
provider even if your settings does not support this.

To make an emergency call from a lock screen, on the Enter
Passcode screen, tap **Emergency** and then dial the required number.

Visual Voicemail

This option allows you to access your voice messages.

Please note that the instructions given below may not be applicable
to you depending on your service provider.

To set up visual voicemail:

1. From the Home screen, tap on **phone app** .

2. Tap on **Voicemail** icon Voicemail .

3. If you are using voicemail for the first time, select **Set Up
   Now**.

4. Enter a 4 to 15-digit voicemail password and select **Done**.

5. Re-enter your voicemail password, and select **Done**.

6. Select a default greeting or record a custom greeting, then select **Done**. If you are selecting **Custom,** tap record to record your personal message and tap **Stop** when you finish. Tap **Save** to save the recorded message.

7. Your Visual Voicemail inbox will be displayed. New messages will appear on the voicemail screen for review and playback. Tap a message to begin playback.

8. To get an info about a contact in voicemail, tap the info icon ⓘ next to the contact.

9. To delete a voicemail message, tap **Delete** while viewing the message.

10. To call back a voicemail contact, tap **Call Back** while viewing the message.

Tip: There are some network providers that enable you to setup a voicemail by tapping **Call Voicemail** and following the prompts.

To access and manage your visual voicemail:

1. From the app grid tap on **phone app** .

2. Tap on **Voicemail** icon Voicemail . You may need to enter a password.

3. Tap on a message you want to listen to.

4. Tap **play icon**.

5. You may also tap on **delete icon** to delete it. When you delete a message, the message goes to Deleted message box.

To permanently delete a message, tap **Deleted messages** and tap **Clear All.** Tap **Clear All** again.

Tip: To change a voicemail password, go to **Settings** **> Phone > Change Voicemail Password**.

Using Call Waiting

Call waiting allows you to get another call while you're already on one.

To enable this feature, please go to **Settings** **> Phone > Call waiting**.

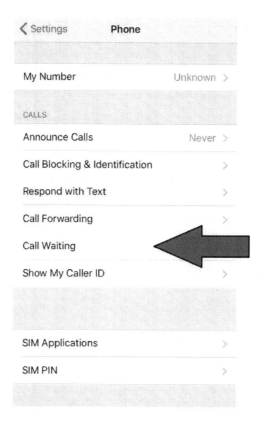

Depending on your network service provider, please note that the screenshot shown above may be different from the one on your device.

Call Forwarding (Diverting Calls to Another Number)

When you are busy, you can forward incoming calls to another phone number. Please note that your network provider will need to support this feature for it to be available.

To enable this feature:

1. From the Home screen, tap **Settings** .

2. Tap **Phone**.

3. Tap **Call Forwarding**.

4. Tap the status switch next to **Call Forwarding** and enter the number you want to forward your calls to.

5. To disable this feature, repeat steps 1 to 3 above and tap the indicator switch next to **Call Forwarding.**

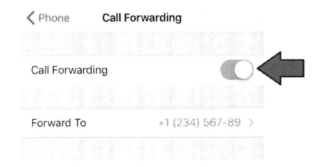

Please note that when the call forwarding option is enabled, you should see the call forwarding icon ↳ on the notification bar at the top of the screen.

In addition, depending on your network provider, you may be able to forward calls to your voice mail and listen to them later.

Block Calls

If your service provider supports this feature, you may be able to avoid receiving calls from certain numbers by using this feature. In addition, the call blocking feature may not affect phone calls made or received via apps (e.g. Skype) installed on your device.

Please note that the features available under Call blocking may differ from one service provider to another.

1. From the Home screen, tap **Settings** .
2. Tap **Phone**.
3. Tap **Call Block & Identification**.
4. Tap **Block Contact....**

5. Tap the contact you would like to block.
6. To unblock a contact, tap **Edit** located at the top of the screen, then tap the minus (-) icon next to the contact and then tap **Unblock.**

Tip: To block calls from an anonymous number or an unknown number, turn on 'Do Not Disturb' manually and set it to allow calls from your contacts list. To learn more about Do Not Disturb, please go page 170.

What about Caller ID?

If your service provider supports this feature, you may prevent your service provider from displaying your number(ID) when you call another person.

1. From the Home screen, tap **Settings** .
2. Tap **Phone**.
3. Tap **Show My Caller ID** and then disable or enable this feature.

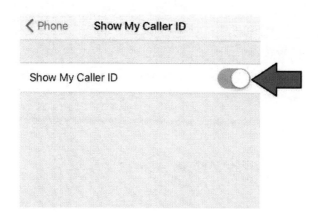

Using the Messaging App

This app allows you to send text, photo, and video messages to other SMS and MMS devices.

Starting/Managing a Conversation

1. Tap the **Messages** app 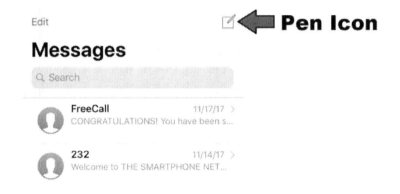 from the Home screen.
2. Tap the new message icon (pen icon) located at the top right corner of the screen.

Edit

⬜️⬅️ Pen Icon

Messages

Q Search

FreeCall   11/17/17 >
CONGRATULATIONS! You have been s...

232   11/14/17 >
Welcome to THE SMARTPHONE NET...

3. Tap the **"To:"** field and type in the first letters of the recipient's name. Your device filters as you type. Then tap the required contact. Note, depending on your service provider, you can add up to 10 contacts (if not more).

4. Tap the text entry field and write the text for your SMS/MMS.

Message field

5. When you are done, tap the Send icon.

 **Send Icon**

6. You can reply a message by tapping on the message and then enter a message in the **Message** field. Tap Send icon when you are done. Please note that if enabled, the messages sent to other iOS devices are sent as iMessages, while non-iOS devices will receive standard text or picture messages. To learn more about iMessage, please see the **hints** on page 123.

7. To delete an entire message thread, tap **Edit** located at the top of the screen. Tap the threads you wish to delete. Tap **Delete.** You can also swipe left on a conversation, then tap **Delete**.

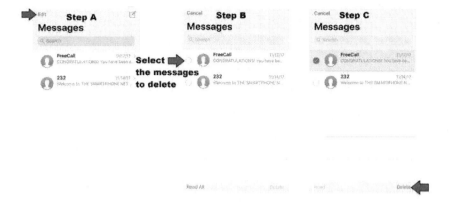

8. To delete a single message from within a thread, tap the thread, press and hold the massage in question and tap on **More...** Tap the message you want to delete, and tap **Delete** 🗑 (located at the bottom left of the screen).

Hints:

- If enabled, if you are sending a message to a contact with an iOS device, the message will be sent as an iMessage. An iMessage uses Wi-Fi or cellular data to send messages. If you would like to enable/disable iMessage, from the Home screen, tap **Settings** > **Messages.** Then tap the status switch next to **iMessages.**

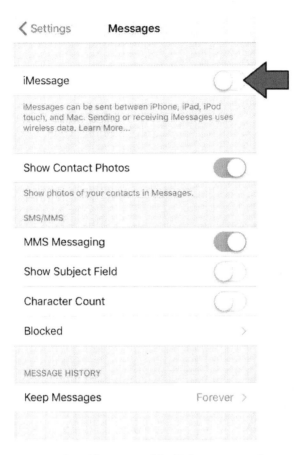

Please note that if you enable iMessage, make sure you also enable **Send as SMS.** This will enable you to send message as SMS when iMessage is unavailable.

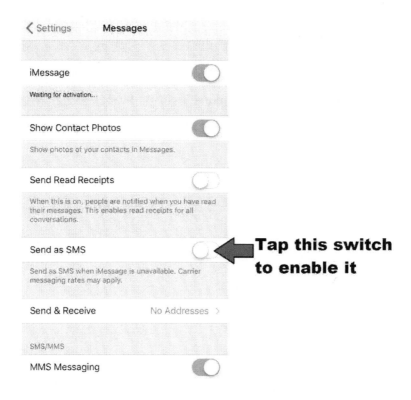

- You can know whether a message will be sent as an iMessage or as an ordinary message. To know this, check what is written on top of the screen when you are about to send the message (after selecting a contact). If **New iMessage** is written, then an iMessage should be sent to the supported devices.

- If you receive an attachment, you can tap on the attachment to view it. Then tap the attachment again and tap ⬆️ .Tap **Save Image**.

- **You can block text messages** from certain numbers if your service provider supports this feature. To do this, from the

Home screen, tap **Settings** > **Messages** > **Blocked**.

Then tap **Add New...** and select contact to block. To unblock

a contact, tap **Edit** located at the top of the screen. Then tap

the red minus (-) icon next to the contact you want to

unblock. Thereafter, select **Unblock**.

EMAIL APP

Introduction

iPhone 8, iPhone 8 Plus or iPhone X comes preloaded with a Mail app for sending and receiving emails and one of the things you will need to do when you start using your device is to set up an email account.

How to Add Your Email Accounts to the Mail App

You probably have many email accounts and you may wish to add these accounts to the Mail app on your device.

The email accounts you can add to the Mail app include Google Mail, Yahoo Mail, iCloud, Exchange, Outlook among others.

To add an email account:

- From the Home screen, tap **Settings** .
- Scroll down and tap **Accounts & Passwords**.
- Tap **Add Account**.
- Tap an account and enter your email address and the password.

- Select your preference and tap **Save**.

- After the setup, open the Mail ✉ app from the Home screen.

Special Note on Adding Exchanged Account to Email App

Following the instructions above might not be enough when you want to add your exchanged account to the Mail app and you may need extra information. You may need to obtain from your Exchange administrator or provider the account's server address, domain name, and username in addition to your email address and password.

Choosing a Default Email Account for Your iPhone

If you have more than one email account configured on your mobile phone, you may need to select a default email account.

- From the Home screen, tap **Settings** ⚙.
- Scroll down and tap **Mail**.
- Tap **Default Account**.

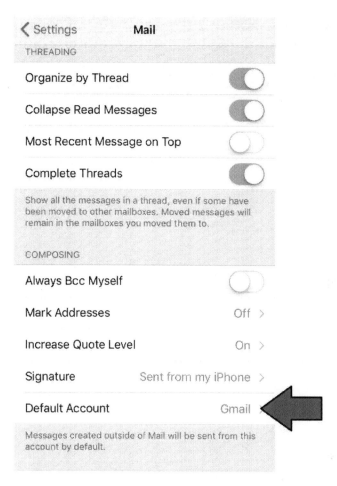

- Tap an email account that you want to make the default from the list of email accounts.

How to Compose and Send an Email Message Using the Mail App

You can easily send an email message to your friends or organization using the Mail App. In this section of the guide, we will be exploring how to compose an email message, and how to send an email message.

To send an email message:

- To send or receive email, from the Home screen, tap **Mail**

- Tap the **compose icon** (the pen icon).

1 — ⟨ Mailboxes   Edit — **2**

All Inboxes

Q Search

4 — ⊜   Updated Just Now   ✎ — **3**
                    6,557 Unread

1. **Account Name:** Tap this to get access to switch from one account to another. This is only applicable if you have multiple email accounts configured on your device. In addition, when you tap this icon, you will get access to different folders under your email account.

2. **Edit:** Tap to delete, move or mark multiple messages.

3. **Compose:** Tap to compose a new message.

4. **Filter:** Tap to filter your messages according to the read, unread etc.

- Tap the field next to **"To:"** and type in the email address of the recipient.

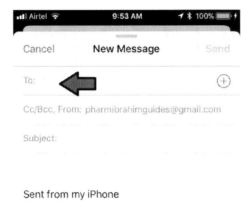

- To send a copy to another person, tap **CC/Bcc** field and type the person's email address in the **Cc/Bcc** field.

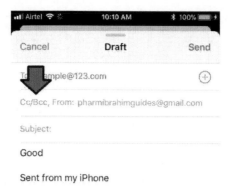

Tip: Cc means Carbon Copy. If you use the Cc option to send a message to many recipients, all the recipients will see the message and all other email addresses that have received the message. On the other hand, Bcc stands for Blind Carbon Copy. If you use the Bcc option to send a message to many recipients, all the recipients will see the message, but will not see other email addresses that have received the message.

- Tap **Subject** and key in the required subject.
- Tap the text input field and write the text for your email.

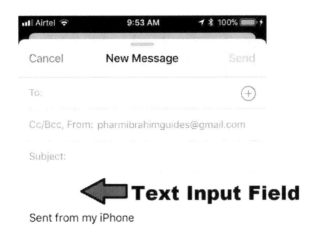

Text Input Field

Sent from my iPhone

- To access more info, tap and hold a blank area in the message field and then choose an option.

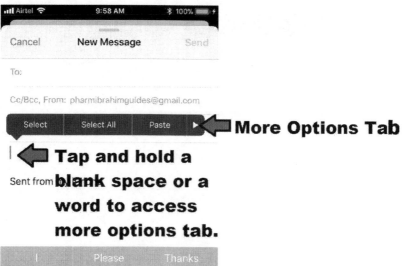

More Options Tab

 **Tap and hold a blank space or a word to access more options tab.**

To access more options while using the more options tab, tap the right facing arrow ▶.

- To bold, italicize or underline a text, tap and hold the text and tap the right facing arrow ▶. Then tap the **BIU** icon and select bold, italic or underline.

- When you are satisfied with the message and you are ready to send it, tap **Send** located at the top of the Mail app screen.

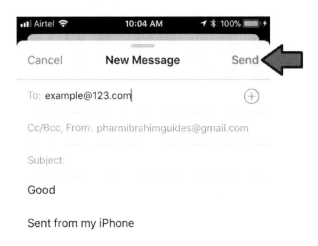

Tip: If you're writing a message and want to finish it later, tap **Cancel** located at the top of the screen, then tap **Save Draft**. To get it back, touch and hold the Compose button ✎ and select the draft message.

Attaching a File

You can insert an attachment into your message. To do this, tap and hold a blank area in the message field and then tap the right facing arrow.

Tap **Add Attachment**. Then locate and tap on the file you want to attach.

Tip: You can group those emails with attachment together under a folder. To do this:

- Open the Mail app and tap **Mailboxes.**

 ‹ Mailboxes   **All Inboxes**   Edit

● **Google Alerts**   12:17 PM >
Google Alert - Best place to read
Best place to read As-it-happens update · 25
November 2017 NEWS Mara: Only The Best Wi...

● **eBay**   11:53 AM >
80 NEW: samsung galaxy note 8 unlocked
Buy It Now from $500.00 to $989.99. Or bid on
8 auctions....

- Tap **Edit**.

Edit

Mailboxes

📥 All Inboxes   6560 >

📬 Gmail   2923 >

- Select **Attachment**.

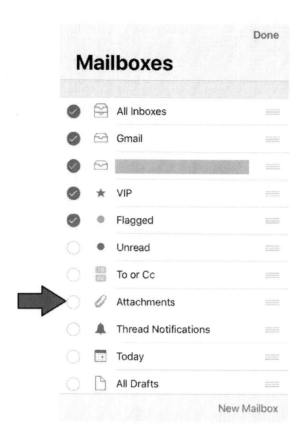

- Tap **Done**.

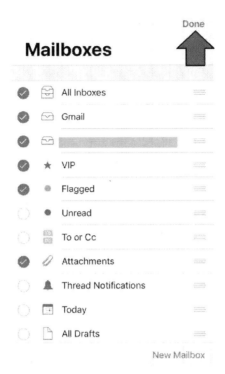

Managing a Received Email

One of the most important functions of any email app is the ability to receive incoming messages. By default, the Mail app searches for new messages and alert you when there is one.

New messages are either stored in Inbox or Junk/Trash/Spam folder and these are the places to check if you are expecting an email.

To read a message or manage a received message:

- Tap on the subject of the message to open the message text in the preview pane.

- The attachment icon (a paperclip icon) means that a message has an attachment.

- To change the email account/ inbox view, tap the back icon at the upper left corner of the screen.

- To reply a message, tap 🔄 and then tap **Reply**. When you tap the reply button, a new window appears. This window is similar to what appears when you tap on new email button but with a slight difference. This window already contains the recipient's name and the subject.

- To forward a message, tap 🔄 and then tap **Forward.** Use this option to send a copy of an email in your inbox to your friends or associates. When you tap on the Forward button, a message window with a subject line preceded by "Fwd:" appears. The original subject, and text are also included. In addition, you will have the option to fill in the email address of the person to whom you are sending the message.

- To archive or delete an email, swipe the email from right to left.

Tip: Get to know the various options available when reading a message in your inbox.

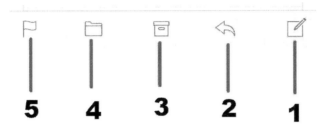

1. Tap this icon to compose a new email message.
2. Tap this icon to reply the current email you are viewing.
3. Tap this icon to archive or thrash an email message.
4. Tap this icon to move a message to a new mailbox/folder. For example, you can use this method to move a message to Starred folder. To do this, simply tap this icon and then tap **Starred**.
5. Tap this icon to flag a message, mark a message as Unread, Move a message to Junk, or get a notification when anyone replies to the message thread you are currently viewing.

How to Open and Save an Attachment in the Mail App

The email with an attachment will have a paper clip icon displayed next to the address of the sender when you check your message inbox.

To open an attachment:

1. Tap the message that has the attachment, as indicated by a paper clip.

2. When the message opens, tap the attachment that you want to open.

3. To save an attachment, tap the attachment again and tap ⬆️ . Then tap **Save...**

Tip: To see only messages with attachments, tap the Filter Messages button ⊜ (located at the bottom left of the screen) to turn on filtering, then tap **Filtered by** and select **Only Mail with Attachments**.

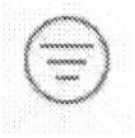

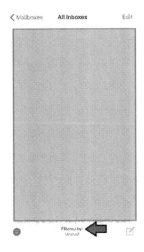

Switch on
this option

Managing the Email Settings

- From the Home screen, tap **Settings** .

- Scroll down and tap **Mail**.

- Tap an option to customize.

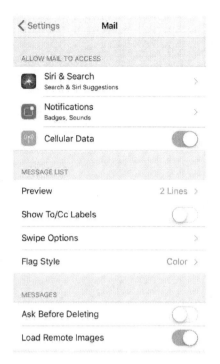

Mail App Options

Deleting an Email Account

- From the Home screen, tap **Settings** .

- Scroll down and tap **Accounts & Passwords**.

- Tap the required email account.

- Tap **Delete Account**.

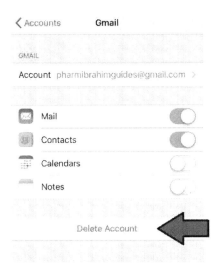

- Tap **Delete from My iPhone**.

How to Remove the Default Email Signature in Email App

You can use the Signature setting to tell Mail app what signature to include in a message.

- From the Home screen, tap **Settings** .
- Scroll down and tap **Mail**.
- Scroll down and tap **Signature**.
- Tap the current signature and adjust it as you like.

Note: An email signature is a text that appears by default after the body of your message. You may set your email signature to be your name or your brand.

Personal Information

Contacts

This app allows you to create and manage a list of your personal or business contacts. You can save names, mobile phone numbers, home phone numbers, email address, and more.

Creating a Contact

1. While on the Home screen, swipe from right to left and tap **Extras**.

2. Tap on **Contacts** app.

3. Tap on + located at the upper right corner of the screen.

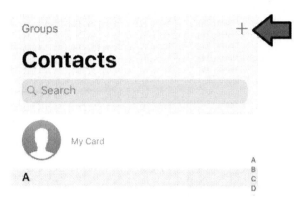

4. Fill in the details by tapping on each item on the screen.

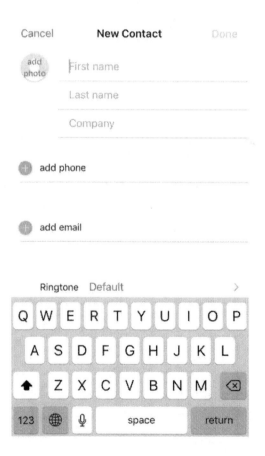

5. When you are done, tap **Done** located at the top of the screen.

Hint: To search for a contact, open the contact app and tap the search bar located at the top of the screen, then start typing a name. The list filters as you write.

You can add a recent caller to your Contacts. To do this, from the Home screen, tap **Phone** , tap **Recents** (located at the bottom of the screen), and then tap the More Info button next to the number. Tap **Create New Contact** or **Add to Existing Contact**, and follow the prompts.

Managing a Contact

1. Repeat the first two steps above.
2. Tap on a contact from the list.
3. Tap **EDIT** located at the top of the screen. Enter the new details and tap **Done**.
4. To delete a contact, tap **EDIT** and then tap on **Delete Contact** located at the bottom of the screen.

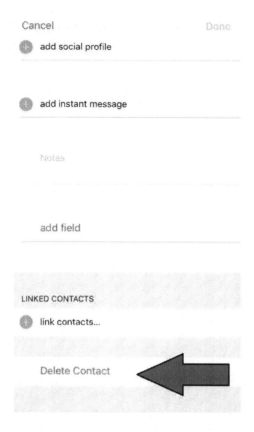

Tip: You can quickly hide all your contacts. To do this, open **Contact** app. Tap **Groups** located at the top of the screen and select **Hide All Contacts.** Tap **Done** to save the changes. To unhide your contacts, follow the similar steps mentioned above and tap **Show All Contacts** and then tap **Done.**

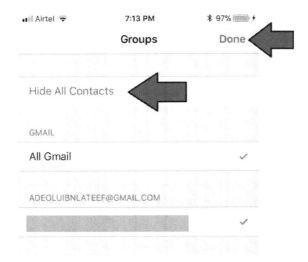

Adding a Contact to Favorites

1. From the Home screen, tap on **Phone** 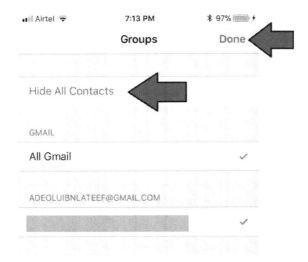 app.

2. Tap the Favorites icon.

No Favorites

3. Tap the Plus sign (+) icon located at the top of the screen.

4. Tap a contact to add to Favorites and select whether you are adding **Message, Call** or **Mail**.

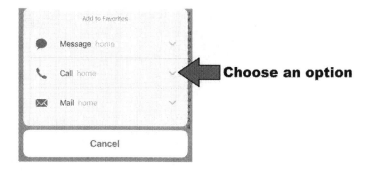

5. To remove a contact from Favorites tab, tap **Edit** located at the top of the screen and then tap the red minus (-) icon next to the contact you want to remove. Then select **Delete.**

Linking Two Contacts

1. While on Home screen, swipe from right to left and tap
   Extras

2. Tap on **Contacts** app.
3. Tap the contact you want to link.
4. Tap **EDIT** located at the top of the screen.
5. Scroll down and tap **Link Contacts...**
6. Tap the required contact.
7. Tap **LINK** located at the top of the screen.

8. Tap **Done** to save the changes.

9. To unlink contacts, tap the contact, tap **Edit** located at the top of the screen. Scroll down to the last item and tap the red minus icon next to the contact you want to unlink. Thereafter, tap **Unlink.** Tap **Done** to save the changes. Please note that unlinking a contact does not delete the contact.

Linking two contacts is important if you have separate entries for the same contact from different social networking services or email accounts.

Hint: To customize the Contact app, from the Home screen, tap on Settings , tap **Contacts** and then select an option.

Importing/Exporting Contacts from One Account to Another

If you have your contacts backup on your email account, you can link this email account to your iPhone so that the contacts can be automatically added to your comtact app.

- From the Home screen, tap **Settings** .
- Scroll down and tap **Accounts & Passwords**.
- Tap **Add Account**.
- Select an account and follow the onscreen instructions to sync your contacts. During the account linking process, please make sure **Contacts** is enabled.

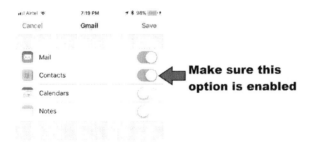

Tip: If you don't enable Contact during the account setup and you wish to enable it at any other time, go to **Settings** > **Account & Passwords.** Then tap the account you want to extract the contacts from. Thereafter, tap the status switch next to **Contacts** to enable contact syncing.

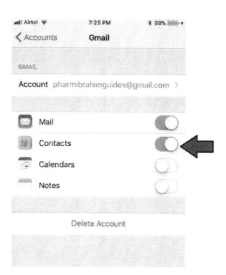

Accessibility Features – the Special Features for Easy Usage

Accessibility features let you customize your device to suit your needs. In addition, it also provides you the opportunity to control your phone in a special way.

A summary of some of Accessibility features is given below.

Tip: To access the Accessibility features, from the Home screen, tap

Settings , tap **General** and then tap **Accessibility.**

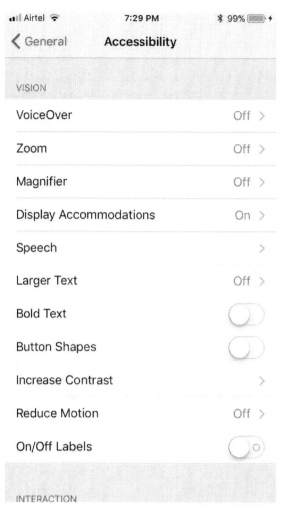

1. **VoiceOver:** This feature reads what you do on the screen aloud making it possible to interact with your device even if you have difficulty seeing the screen.

VoiceOver tells you about each item you select by enclosing the item and describing it.

You can enable VoiceOver by tapping the VoiceOver status switch. When VoiceOver is enabled, you will need to control your screen in a special way to get results.

Basically, you will need to tap the screen to hear the items on the screen or select items. To access the selected item or perform a specific action on the item, double-tap the screen.

2. **Zoom:** This feature allows you to zoom in/out items on the screen. You can enable Zoom by tapping the Zoom status switch. When Zoom is enabled, you can double-tap the screen with three fingers to zoom.

In addition, you can limit the maximum magnification by adjusting the slider under the zoom option.

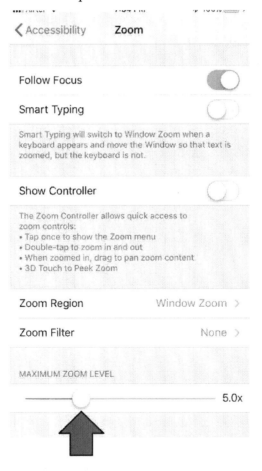

3. **Magnifier:** When this option is enabled, you can use your iPhone to magnify items near you just as you do with magnifying glass. When enabled, triple-click the Home button to start Magnifier. If you are using iPhone X, triple-click the side button to launch the Magnifier.

To exit the Magnifier, press the Home button. On iPhone X, swipe up from the button of the screen to exit the Magnifier.

4. **Display Accommodations:** This option allows you to tweak colors on the screen of your device so as to make the screen easier to read.

5. **Speech:** This option allows you to customize speech related options.

6. **Larger Text:** When this option is enabled, text in some apps are made larger and easier to read. You can use the slider under the **Larger Text** screen to adjust the text size.

7. **Bold Text:** When this option is enabled, text in some apps appear bold and easier to read.

8. **Button Shapes:** When this option is enabled, onscreen buttons should be easier to see.

9. **Increase the Contrast:** You can use this option to increase text contrast where possible.

10. **Reduce Motion:** When this option is enabled, motion due to Siri animations, typing auto completion, bubble and screen effects in Messages may be reduced.

11. **On/Off Labels:** When this option is enabled, additional labels are displayed on on/off switches making it easier to distinguish whether a setting is on or off.

12. **Reachability**: When this option is enabled, you will be able to bring the top of the screen into your reach by tapping (not pressing) the Home button twice. To return the screen to its normal place, double tap home button again. Reachability not supported on iPhone X.

13. **Switch Control:** This feature is particularly good for those with motor impairment. Switch Control let you control your phone using a connected physical switches. I will advise you don't tamper with the **Switch Control** unless you know much about it.

14. **AssistiveTouch**: This option allows you to use your iPhone in a special way. You can use this option to create your own gesture and tell your iPhone what to do when you perform a gesture.

AssistiveTouch is particularly useful when you have difficulty in touching the screen or pressing the buttons.

When AssistiveTouch is on, the floating menu button appears on the screen.

Floating menu

15. **Touch Accommodations**: Use this feature to customize how the screen responds to touches. With this feature, you can configure iPhone to respond only to touches of a certain duration.

16. **Keyboard**: Use this tab to customize virtual keyboard related settings.

17. **Shake to Undo:** When this option is enabled, you should be able to undo an action by shaking your iPhone. Please note that if you are someone that shakes his/her phone frequently then I will advise that you disable this feature to avoid undoing intentional actions.

18. **Call audio routing**: This option allows you to have the audio of incoming or outgoing calls automatically routed through a headset or speaker phone instead of your iPhone.

19. **Home Button**: Use this tab to customize Home button related settings.

20. **LED Flash For Alerts**: When this option is enabled, your device will flash its LED flash light when there is an incoming call or other alerts.

21. **Mono Audio:** This feature allows you to adjust the sound from the left and right channels so that you can hear the sound from your iPhone with either ear.

22. **Subtitles & Captioning:** Use this tab to customize subtitles & captioning related settings.

23. **Audio Description**: When this option is enabled, your iPhone will provide an audible description of video scenes for videos that include audible description.

24. **Guided Access:** This option allows you to restrict your access to some apps/tasks on your phone for a particular time.

25. **Accessibility Shortcuts**: This option lets you turn the accessibility features you use most on and off by triple-clicking the Home button.

Hints: Interestingly, Apple includes descriptions under many Accessibility options, you can read these descriptions to know how to tweak them.

TOOLS

Lower Power Mode

Low Power Mode allows you to conserve battery and use your phone for longer hours. Please note that some process may behave unusually when this mode is enabled. For example, your iPhone may perform some tasks more slowly when this feature is enabled.

To enable and Low Power Mode:

1. From the Home screen, tap **Settings** .
2. Tap **Battery**.
3. Tap the indicator switch next to **Low Power Mode**.

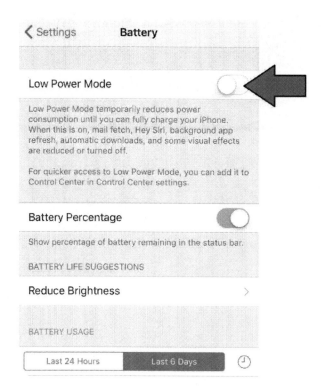

3D Touch

3D Touch gives you some customized experience when you press and hold some items firmly on the screen of your device.

- **Using 3D Touch on the Home Screen:** To use 3D Touch on the Home screen, press and hold an app icon firmly to bring out the app shortcuts. The app shortcut for message app is shown below.

Please note that if you press gently and lightly, the apps will begin to shake instead, and you will not be able to access the 3D Touch options.

- **Using 3D Touch in the Mail App:** To use 3D Touch in the Mail app, press and hold an email message firmly to preview the email then swipe up to bring up options (like the one shown below).

- **Using 3D Touch in the Contact App:** To use 3D Touch in contact app, press and hold a contact firmly to bring up options.

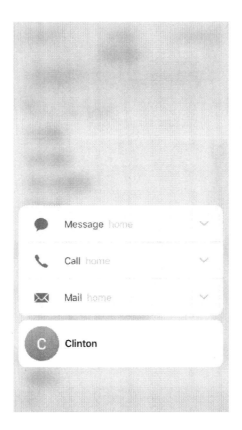

Message home ⌄

Call home ⌄

Mail home ⌄

C Clinton

Do Not Disturb

If you don't want to be disturbed by calls or notifications, you can set your mobile phone to be silent for a specified amount of time.

1. From the Home screen, tap **Settings** .
2. Tap **Do Not Disturb**.
3. To turn on/off **Do Not Disturb,** tap the status switch next to **Do Not Disturb**. Please note that when Do Not Disturb is

enabled, calls and alerts that arrive while locked will be
silenced.

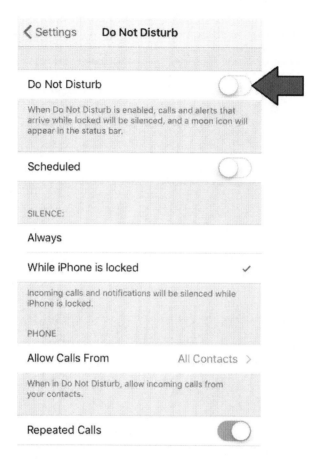

4. To set the time when Do Not Disturb will be active, tap the
   status switch next to **Schedule.**

5. Tap **From** and scroll to the time you would like Do Not
   Disturb to begin.

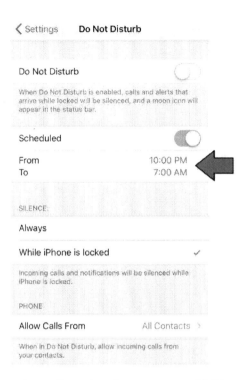

Do Not Disturb

When Do Not Disturb is enabled, calls and alerts that arrive while locked will be silenced, and a moon icon will appear in the status bar.

Scheduled

From   10:00 PM
To   7:00 AM

SILENCE:

Always

While iPhone is locked   ✓

Incoming calls and notifications will be silenced while iPhone is locked.

PHONE

Allow Calls From   All Contacts ›

When in Do Not Disturb, allow incoming calls from your contacts.

6. Tap **To** and scroll to the time you would like Do Not Disturb to end.

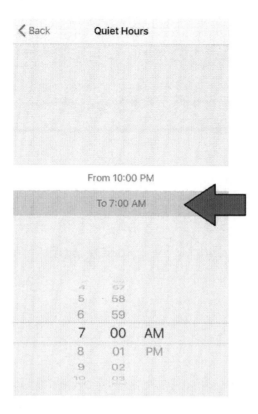

7. Tap **Back** located at the top of the screen to save changes.

8. Tap **Always** if you want to set your mobile phone to silent mode permanently. Tap **Only while iPhone is locked** if you want to set your mobile phone to a silent mode only when the screen lock is turned on.

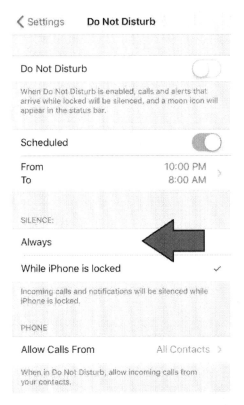

‹ Settings   **Do Not Disturb**

Do Not Disturb

When Do Not Disturb is enabled, calls and alerts that arrive while locked will be silenced, and a moon icon will appear in the status bar.

Scheduled

From   10:00 PM
To   8:00 AM

SILENCE:

Always

While iPhone is locked   ✓

Incoming calls and notifications will be silenced while iPhone is locked.

PHONE

Allow Calls From   All Contacts ›

When in Do Not Disturb, allow incoming calls from your contacts.

9. Tap **Allow Calls From** to choose who is able to call you while Do Not Disturb is turned on. You may choose favorite if you want to receive calls from only your favorites when Do Not Disturb is enabled. To know more about Favorites, please go page 152.

10. To allow your phone to ring aloud (the second time) when the same person calls you two times within three minutes, tap the status switch next to **Repeated Calls.**

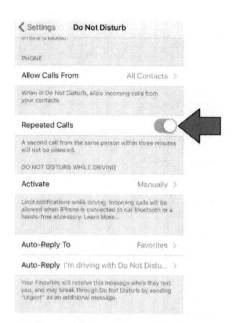

11. To turn **Do Not Disturb** off, swipe up from the bottom of the screen to access Control Center. Then tap **Do Not Disturb** icon. If you are using iPhone X, swipe down from the top-right edge of the screen to access Control Center.

Creating Schedules and More with the Calendar

Your phone provides you with the **Calendar** app to help you organize your schedules and tasks more conveniently and effectively. You can create schedules and add events.

> ➤ **To create an event**

1. From the Home screen, tap on **Calendar** .
2. Tap on + located at the upper right corner of the screen.

3. Fill in the details by tapping on each item on the screen.

4. When you are finished, tap **Add**.

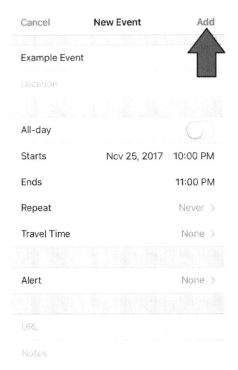

Cancel	New Event	Add

Example Event

Location

All-day

Starts	Nov 25, 2017	10:00 PM

Ends	11:00 PM

Repeat	Never >

Travel Time	None >

Alert	None >

URL

Notes

➤ To edit/share or delete an event alarm

1. From the Home screen, tap on **Calendar** 25.

2. Tap the event date and then tap on the event you want to delete.

3. Tap **Edit** located at the top of the screen.

4. Scroll down and tap **Delete Event**.

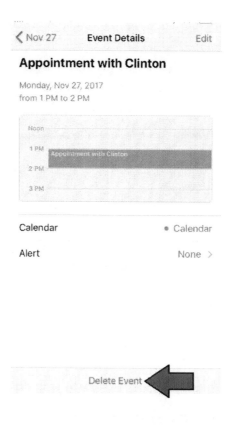

> **To change your calendar view and view events**

1. From the Home screen, tap on **Calendar** 25 .

2. Tap the small back arrow next to the Month to change from day view to month view or from month view to year view.

3. Tap the menu icon to view events.

4. To access day view and see your events, tap **Today** located at the bottom of the screen.

Hint: To search for items on your calendar, tap the search button (lens icon) and begin to type a keyword.

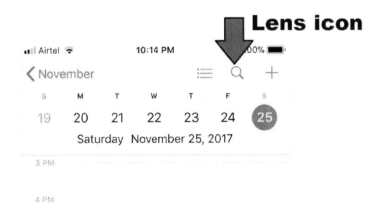

In addition, you can view a weekly calendar by rotating your iPhone sideways.

To customize calendar settings, from the Home screen, tap **Settings** , tap **Calendar** and choose an option.

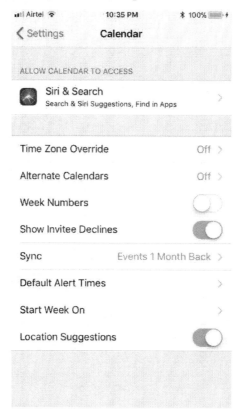

Tip: If you want your Google Calendar to be sync with your iPhone, go to **Settings** > **Account & Passwords.** Then tap your Google account and tap the status switch next to **Calendars** to enable calendar syncing.

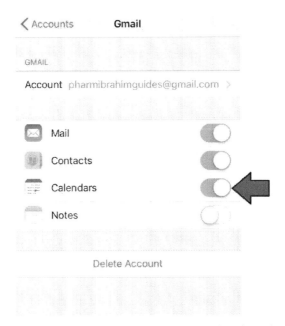

You can also use this above method to sync calendars from other account(s).

In the tip above, please note that I assumed that you have already linked your Google account, if you have not, then go to **Settings** 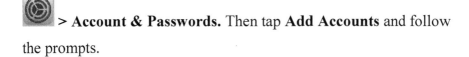 > **Account & Passwords.** Then tap **Add Accounts** and follow the prompts.

Using the Camera

iPhone 8, iPhone 8 Plus and iPhone X come with rear-facing camera, front-facing camera and LED flash. With these cameras, you can capture a photo or record a video.

Note: The memory capacity of the picture taken may differ depending on the settings, shooting scene and shooting conditions.

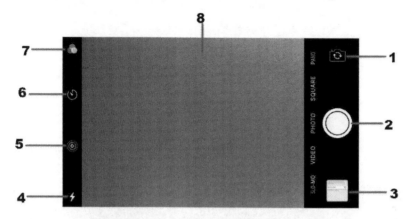

Number	Function
1.	Front-facing/rear-facing camera switch.
2.	Camera/Video button (Shutter button).
3.	Preview thumbnail tab.
4.	**Flash icon**: Use this button to activate or deactivate the flash.
5.	Live Image button. This is used to capture what happens just before you take a picture and after you take a picture. This can be used to capture a moving scene.
6.	Photo Timer.
7.	Choose a Filter.
8.	Picture Pane.

➢ **To Capture a photo**

1. From the Home screen tap **Camera** .

2. If necessary, swipe to PHOTO

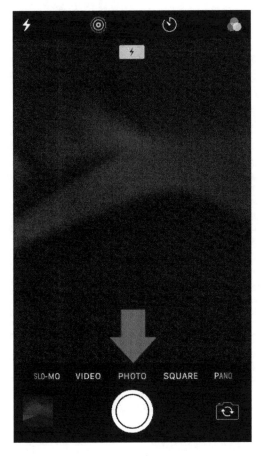

3. Aim the lens at the subject and make any necessary adjustments. To focus any part of the screen, tap that part of the screen.

3. Tap **front-facing/rear-facing icon** to switch between the rear-facing and front-facing camera.

4. To zoom in, place two fingers on the screen and spread them apart. Do the reverse to zoom out.

5. To add a filter, tap the **Filter icon** . Then tap the filter you would like to use.

6. To capture a moving scene/live scene, tap and then tap the shutter button.

7. Tap on **camera button** ⭕ when you are done adjusting the settings.

To customize camera settings:
Unfortunately, you have to leave the camera app to access its settings.

1. From the Home screen, tap **Settings** 🎛️.
2. Scroll down and tap **Camera**.
3. Tap an option.

Hint: Camera settings consist of quite a number of features, you may not need to touch some of the features. In fact, the default settings are enough for many users.

Using Photo Timer
Photo timer allows you to tell your device when to automatically take a picture.
To use this option:

• From the Home screen tap **Camera** 🎛️.

- Tap the timer icon 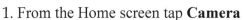, choose 3s or 10s and then tap the shutter button .

- Then wait for the camera to take the picture after the countdown.

Recording a Video

1. From the Home screen tap **Camera** .

2. Swipe to **Video**.

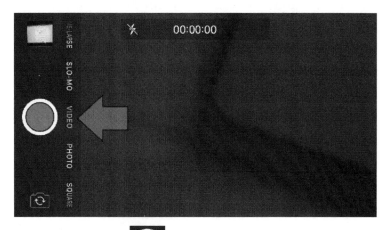

3. Tap the **video button** .

4. When done with the recording, tap the **video button** again.

5. To view your recorded videos, go to Photos app.

Tip: To delete an image, from the Home Screen, go to **Photos,** tap the image you want to delete and tap the delete 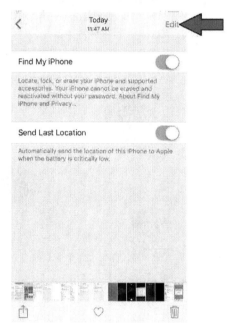 icon located at the bottom of the screen.

To edit an image, tap the image, then tap **Edit** located at the top of the screen and pick an editing tool. When you are done editing, tap **Done** located at the bottom of the screen.

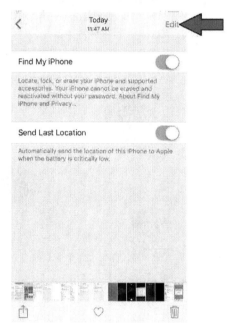

Connectivity

Computer Connections

Your phone can be connected to a computer with a USB cable. This will enable you to transfer files such as audio files, video files, document files and image files to your phone from your computer.

Warning: Do not disconnect the USB cable from a computer while the device is transferring or accessing the data. This may result in data loss.

Transferring content via USB

Note: If you have not done so before, you may need to install iTunes on your computer before you transfer contents. To install iTunes, please visit this link **https://www.apple.com/itunes/download**
If your computer is a Windows computer, please ensure you are using windows 7 or later and that you are using iTunes 12.5 or later. You can get most recent iTunes by following the link above.

To Transfer content via USB:
1. Connect your device to a computer with a Lightning to USB cable.
2. iTunes should launch automatically. If it does not, you will need to open it by clicking on its icon on your computer.

3. Tap **Trust** when prompted. You may also need to enter your passcode.

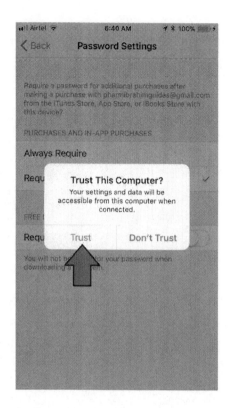

4. When prompted on your computer, tap continue.

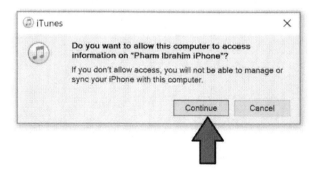

5. If you are using your phone for the first time on iTune, follow the onscreen instructions on your computer to set it up.

6. Click the iPhone icon located at the top of the screen.

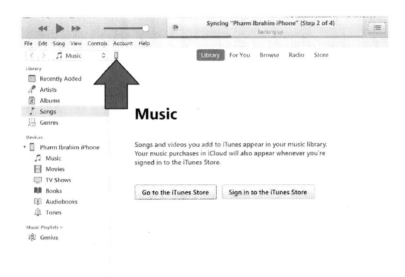

7. If not already selected, click on **Summary.**

8. Scroll down and select **Sync with this iPhone over Wi-Fi.**
Click on **Done.** If prompted, select **Apply.** You may need to
click on the iPhone icon at the top of the screen after
applying the changes.

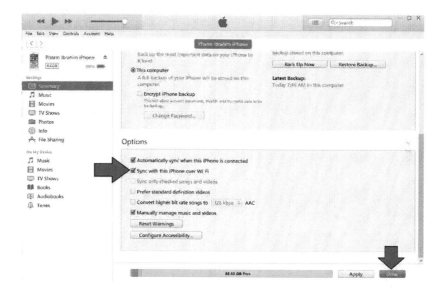

Please note that selecting this option will make your iPhone to
automatically sync when it is plugged in to power, iTunes app is
opened on your computer, and your iPhone and computer are on the
same Wi-Fi network.

9. To backup content from iTunes to a new iPhone, click on
Restore Backup and follow the prompts.

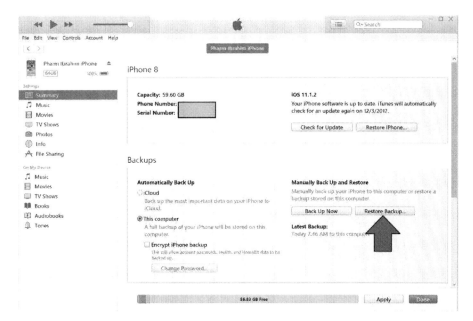

10. To sync a content with your computer, select the content category and select **Sync...** (usually located at the top of the screen). Select what you want to sync and click **Apply** located at the bottom of the screen.

11. Disconnect your phone by removing the USB cable from your computer/iPhone when you are done.

Tip: To transfer files such as images from your iPhone to your computer, connect your iPhone to your computer as described above and then open **Photos** on your PC and then click on **Import**.

Then select **From a USB device.** Then click on **Continue.** Read the onscreen instructions and click on **Import.**

Alternatively, to access the images on your device, just go to **This PC** and click on the name of your iPhone. Then click on **Internal Storage > DCIM > 100APPLE**

Note: The process of file transfer described above is based on Windows 10 PC, if you are using Mac computer or Windows 7 or 8, then there may be some differences.

Wi-Fi

Using your phone, you can connect to the internet or other network devices anywhere an access point or wireless hotspot is available.

To activate the Wi-Fi feature and connect to a network:

1. From the Home screen, tap **Settings** .
2. Tap **Wi-Fi**.
3. Tap the switch next to Wi-Fi to turn it on.

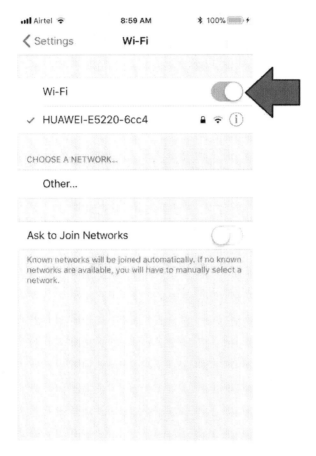

4. Your device then automatically scans for available networks and displays them.

5. Select a network.

6. Enter a password for the network (if necessary) and tap **Join.**

7. To turn Wi-Fi off, from the Home screen, tap **Settings** > **Wi-Fi** and then tap the status switch. Alternatively, swipe up from the bottom of the screen and tap Wi-Fi icon . If

you are using iPhone X, swipe down from the top-right edge

of the screen to access Wi-Fi icon .

Notes:

- The Wi-Fi feature running in the background will consume battery. To save battery, put it off whenever you are not using it.

- The Wi-Fi may not connect a network if the network signal is not good.

- When Wi-Fi is active, the **Wi-Fi** icon is displayed on the status bar.

Tips:

To be notified when a Wi-Fi network is available, turn on **Ask to Join Networks**.

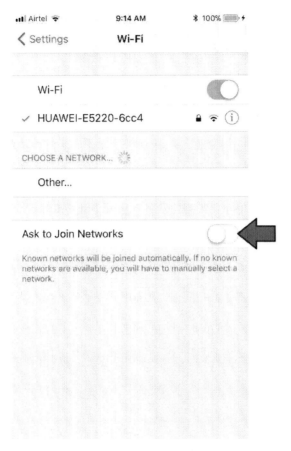

To adjust the settings for a particular Wi-Fi network, tap the info

icon ⓘ next to the Wi-Fi network. For example, to forget a

network, just tap this info ⓘ icon and tap **Forget This Network**.

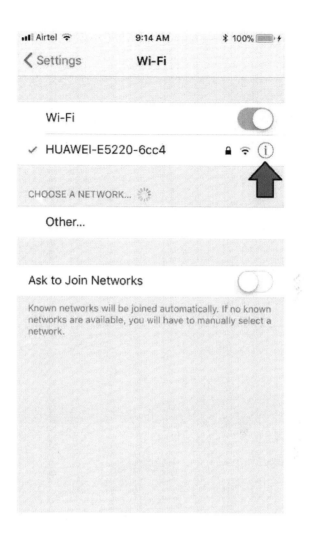

Turning Mobile Data On/Off for Specific Apps

If you are very concerned about saving your data, you can prevent some apps from using your mobile data. In addition, turning off apps may help save battery life.

1. From the Home screen, tap **Settings** .

2. Tap **Cellular.**

3. Tap the status switch next to **Cellular Data** to enable this feature.

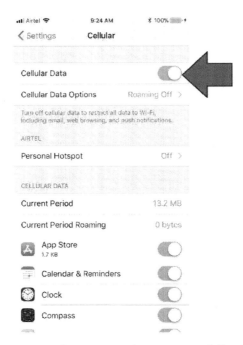

4. To prevent apps from accessing your mobile data, scroll down and tap the status switch next to the individual app.

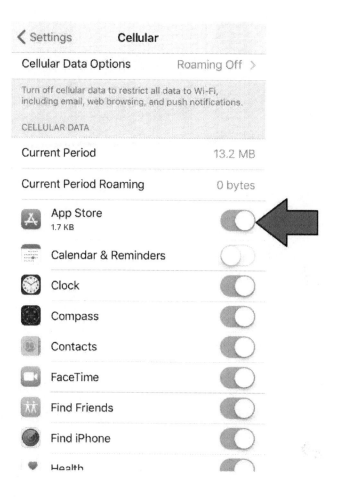

Depending on your network service provider, please note that the screenshot shown above may be different from the one on your device.

Tip: To quickly switch off cellular data, swipe up from the bottom of the screen and tap cellular data icon ![icon]. If you are using iPhone X, swipe down from the top-right edge of the screen to access cellular data icon ![icon].

Using Your Phone as a Hotspot

If your network provider supports it, you can use this feature to share your mobile network with friends.

1. From the Home screen, tap **Settings** .
2. Tap **Cellular**.
3. Tap **Personal Hotspot**.
4. Tap the status switch next to **Personal Hotspot**.

5. Read the onscreen connection instructions to know how to connect devices to your iPhone.

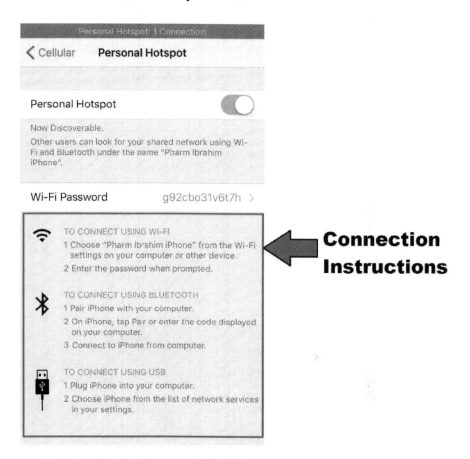

6. Tap the field next to **Wi-Fi Password** and enter a memorable password for the network and then tap **Done**. This is the password that must be entered on other devices wishing to connect to your Personal Hotspot.

7. To change the name of your device, from the Home screen, tap **Settings**  > **General** > **About** > **Name**.

8. After enabling Personal Hotspot, your friends should be able to connect to it just like they connect to other wireless networks.

9. To turn off personal hotspot, from the Home screen, tap **Settings** > **Cellular** > **Personal Hotspot** and then tap the status switch.

Access More by Using Bluetooth

Bluetooth option allows you to connect to another Bluetooth device within range.

Note: If there are obstacles, the operating distance of the Bluetooth may be reduced. The Bluetooth communication range is usually approximately 33 feet.

To use the Bluetooth feature:

1. From the Home screen, tap **Settings** .
2. Tap **Bluetooth**.
3. Next to **Bluetooth**, tap the status switch.
4. Then Bluetooth automatically scans for nearby Bluetooth devices and displays them.
5. Tap a device to connect with. You may need to enter a passcode. For many devices, the PIN is usually 0000 or 1234. Tap **Pair**.

6. When active, a **Bluetooth icon** ⁎ will appear on the status bar. Pairing between two Bluetooth devices is usually a one-time process. Once two devices are paired, the devices continue to recognize this association and you may not need to re-enter a passcode.

7. To turn **Bluetooth** off, from the Home screen, tap **Settings** 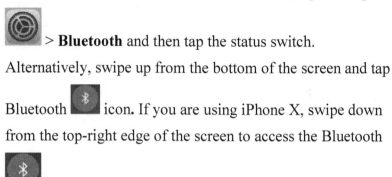 > **Bluetooth** and then tap the status switch. Alternatively, swipe up from the bottom of the screen and tap Bluetooth icon. If you are using iPhone X, swipe down from the top-right edge of the screen to access the Bluetooth icon.

Unpairing a Paired Device

1. From the Home screen, tap **Settings** 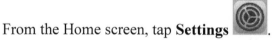.
2. Tap **Bluetooth**.
3. Next to **Bluetooth**, tap the status switch.

4. Tap the info ⓘ icon next to the paired device, and then tap **Forget This Device** to unpair the paired device.

Location Services

Enabling location service allows Map and other apps to serve you content related services.

To activate location services:

1. From the Home screen, tap **Settings** .

2. Scroll down and tap **Privacy**.

3. Tap **Location Services**.

4. Tap the status switch next to the **Location Services**.

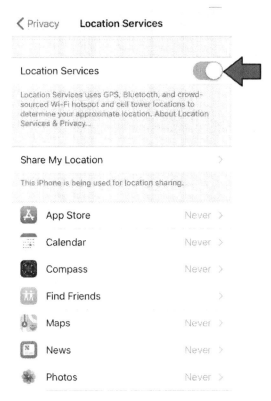

5. To prevent apps from accessing your location, tap the individual app under **Share My Location** and choose **Never**.

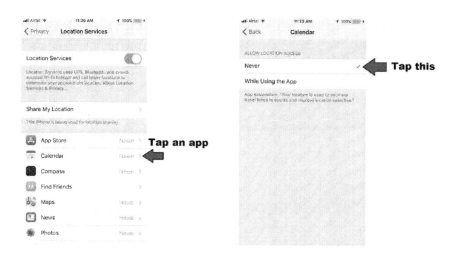

Note: When an app is using Location Services, the Location Services icon appears on the status bar.

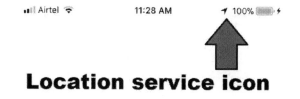

Location service icon

Find My iPhone

You can use this feature to locate your phone if lost.

Note: Find My iPhone must be turned on before your iPhone is lost. To do this:

1. From the Home screen, tap **Settings** .

2. Tap on your account name (in this case, it is **Pharm Ibrahim**).

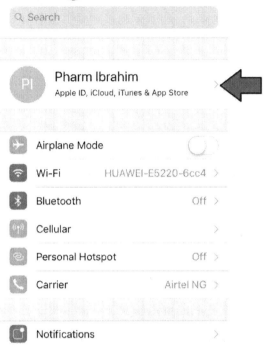

Settings

Q Search

Pharm Ibrahim
Apple ID, iCloud, iTunes & App Store

Airplane Mode

Wi-Fi   HUAWEI-E5220-6cc4 >

Bluetooth   Off >

Cellular   >

Personal Hotspot   Off >

Carrier   Airtel NG >

Notifications   >

3. Tap **iCloud**.

4. Scroll down and tap **Find My iPhone.** Then tap the status switch to activate this feature.

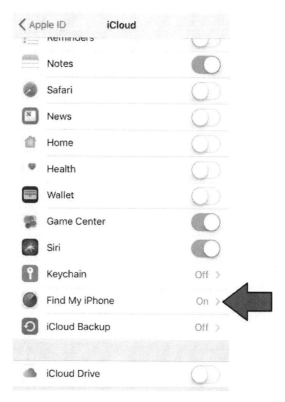

Also, if you want Apple to note the last location of your phone when the battery is low, enable the status switch next to **Send Last Location**

To find you lost phone:

1. Open a web browser and go to **https://www.icloud.com/find**

2. Enter your Apple ID and password. Then click the small arrow icon.

Sign in to iCloud

pharmibrahimguides@gmail.com

●●●●●●●●●●●●●●●

☐ Keep me signed in

Forgot Apple ID or password?

Don't have an Apple ID? Create yours now.

3. If necessary, click **Find My iPhone.**

4. Click **All Devices** and click your phone name. Then your iPhone's current location will be displayed on the map. You can also select other options like erasing your iPhone, turning on lost mode, or ringing your phone. **Lost mode** allows you to display a phone number on the phone so that people can reach you using that number. To activate lost mode, simply click on **Lost Mode** and follow the prompts.

Please note that your lost phone may need to be connected to the internet for you to access its current location.

Settings

Settings menu give you the opportunity to customize your device as you like.

To access the settings menu:

1. From the Home screen, tap **Settings** .
2. Tap a setting category.

Search for Settings

It is advisable to use the searching feature when you are not sure exactly where to find a certain setting.

1. From the Home screen, tap **Settings** .
2. Tap **Search**.

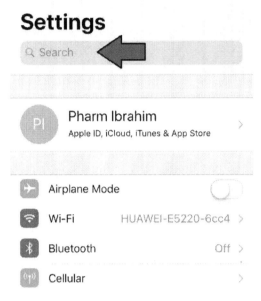

Settings

Q Search

Pharm Ibrahim
Apple ID, iCloud, iTunes & App Store >

Airplane Mode

Wi-Fi   HUAWEI-E5220-6cc4 >

Bluetooth   Off >

Cellular   >

3. Enter a search phrase in the Search field. The list filters as you write.

4. Tap an option (make sure you select the best match).

Hint: There is a tip to getting what you want from your device. From time to time, you will want to customize your phone in a special way. All you need to do in a period like this is to open the Settings as described above. Then tap the search tab and enter a search word relating to what you want to do.

What You Must Know About iPhone 8/iPhone 8 Plus/iPhone X

How to Find Your Phone When lost

As a human being, it is not impossible that you may misplace your phone. If someone else (a thief) has not taken custody of it, there are steps to follow to find it. These steps have been discussed at length in the preceding chapter; please refer to page 205 for details.

How to Reduce Your Mobile Data Usage on iPhone 8/iPhone 8 Plus/iPhone X

If you realize that you are using more MB/Data than normal, there are steps to follow to reduce your data consumption.

1. The first thing is to make sure that you update apps on Wi-Fi only. You can configure this by going to the settings under individual app.

2. Monitor/limit your data usage: To do this, please go to page 197. In addition, there are many applications on Apple store allowing you to monitor your data usage. Knowing how you use your data will enable you to figure out what to do.

How to Conserve iPhone 8, iPhone 8 Plus, or iPhone X Battery Life

You may notice that you have to charge iPhone 8, iPhone 8 Plus or iPhone X twice a day in order to keep the phone on. There are steps to follow to ensure that your phone serves you throughout the day with just a single charge.

1. **Reduce the screen brightness:** I have realized over time that screen brightness consumes a lot of energy. There is usually a substantial difference between using a phone with a maximum brightness and using it with a moderate brightness. As a rule, don't use your phone with a maximum brightness unless you can't see what is on the screen clearly. For example, if you are outdoor. And please make sure you reduce it immediately when it is no more needed. To reduce the screen brightness, tap **Settings** > **Display & Brightness**. Then use the slider under **BRIGHTNESS** to adjust the screen brightness.

2. **Shorten the Screen timeout:** If you really want to save your battery, you must try to shorten the screen timeout. Reducing how long your phone will stay lit up after you finish interacting with it will really help you to save battery. To

manage the screen timeout settings, tap **Settings** 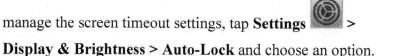 >
Display & Brightness > Auto-Lock and choose an option.

3. **Turn off Wi-Fi and Bluetooth:** When you are not using Wi-
   Fi or Bluetooth, please always remember to put them off.
   These features really consume energy and they are better off
   when not in use.

4. **Use a correct charger:** Using wrong charger can endanger
   the health of your phone/battery, and it is better to avoid such
   practice.

5. **Consider switching off your phone:** If you are not going to
   use your phone for an extended period, you may consider
   switching off your phone.

6. **Use headphones:** Using the headphones is another cool way
   to save your battery. Extended use of audio speakers of your
   phone may drain your battery faster.

How to Take Screenshot on Your iPhone

Another task you can perform on your device is taking a screenshot.
To take a screenshot with your device, please follow the instructions
below:

While at the exact screen you want to capture, press and hold the Home key and the Side button simultaneously. You should hear a short sound when the screenshot is captured. You can view captured images in **Photos** app.

Note: *To take a screenshot on iPhone X, simultaneously press the side button and the volume up button together.*

Extras

What You Must Do Before Selling or Giving away Your iPhone 8, iPhone 8 Plus or iPhone X

Please if you are planning to sell or give away your iPhone, make sure you completely erase your data on it.

To completely erase your data:

1. From the Home screen, tap **Settings** .
2. Tap on your account name (in this case, it is **Pharm Ibrahim**).

3. Scroll down and tap **Sign Out**. Tap **Sign Out** again when
    prompted. To back up your information before you sign out,
    tap **iCloud > iCloud Backup > Back Up Now**.

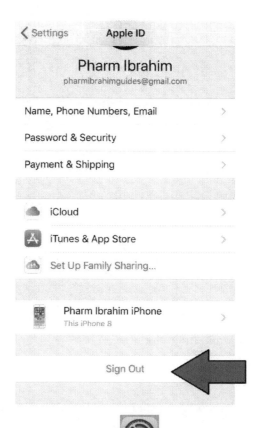

4. Then go back to **Settings** .

5. Tap **General**.

6. Tap **Reset**.

7. Tap **Erase All Content and Settings.** If prompted to enter your Apple ID and password, enter it.

8. Tap **Erase iPhone** and follow the prompts to complete the erasing process.

Please note that if you decide not to sell your iPhone again, you will need to set it up all over again. In addition, features like **Find My iPhone** (see page 205) may be turned off when you perform a complete reset.

Safety Precautions When Using iPhone 8, iPhone 8 Plus or iPhone X on Wi-Fi

With many free Wi-Fi hotspots, it is likely that you are going to find yourself using Wi-Fi more on your phone. There are few things to keep in mind when using Wi-Fi.

1. Confirm the Network Name

Hackers sometimes set up a fake Wi-Fi network in order to tap into the information of unwitting public users. To avoid this, make sure you are sure of the name of the network you are connecting to. You may ask any trusted individual around you if you doubt the name of a network.

2. Connect to a Secured Site

Whenever you are sending a sensitive information always make sure that the site is a secured website. You can know whether a website is a secured site or not by checking whether the url address of the website starts with **HTTPS.** If it starts with https, then it should be a secured site.

3. Get a Virtual Private Network (VPN)

It is highly important you use a virtual private network when using a public network. There are both free and paid VPN providers.

4. Avoid Automatic Connection

Make sure your Wi-Fi is off when not using it to avoid your phone automatically connecting to an open network. Turning your Wi-Fi off when not using it will also save your battery.

I am Having a Dwindling Love for My iPhone 8, iPhone 8 Plus or iPhone X; What Should I do?

It is possible that after buying iPhone 8, iPhone 8 Plus or iPhone X, you realize that it performs below your expectation. It is likely that you dislike your phone because of its hardware or software issue. Generally, the hardware has to do with the design, the phone make up, the weight of the phone etc. while the software has to do with OS and applications.

If your love for iPhone 8, iPhone 8 Plus or iPhone X is reducing because of the software, there is a way out. You can take time to look for beneficial apps to install on your device.

If your love for iPhone 8, iPhone 8 Plus or iPhone X is reducing because of the hardware then it is either you learn how to live with it (you may have to force yourself to love it) or you sell it. If you are considering selling your phone, then make sure you read page 217 before selling it.

Troubleshooting

If the touch screen responds slowly or improperly or your phone is not responding, try the following:

- Remove any protective covers (screen protector) from the touch screen.
- Ensure that your hands are clean and dry when tapping.
- Press the power button once to lock the screen and press it again to unlock the screen and enter a PIN/password if required or press the Touch ID.
- Switch off your device and turn it on again.

Your Phone Doesn't Charge

- Make sure you are using the recommended Apple charger to charge your phone.
- If the iPhone 8, iPhone 8 Plus or iPhone X does not indicate that it is charging, unplug the power adapter, switch off your phone and switch it on again.
- Make sure you are using the USB cable that came with the iPhone 8, iPhone 8 Plus or iPhone X or anyone that has similar specs.

Your device is hot to the touch

When you use applications that require more power or use applications on your device for an extended period of time, your phone may be a bit hot to touch. This is normal, and it should not affect performance. You may just allow your phone to rest for some time or close some applications.

Your phone freezes or has a fatal error

If your phone freezes or it is unresponsive and refuses to power off, press and release the volume up button, press and release the volume down button and then press and hold the side button until your mobile phone restarts.

Phone does not have cellular data network

Make sure you don't have a limited network connectivity in that area. If your network is good and you still don't have cellular network, then make sure the Airplane mode is off. To check whether Airplane mode is enabled, swipe up from the bottom edge of the screen. If you are using iPhone X, swipe down from the top-right edge of the screen. Airplane mode icon will appear colored when enabled/on. Please note that the Airplane mode should be disabled/off to access cellular networks.

Phone does not connect to Wi-Fi

- Try restarting the Wi-Fi.

- Move closer to your router, turn off and turn on Wi-Fi again.

- Restart your router and modem. Unplug the modem and router for few minutes and plug the modem in and then the router.

- Try restarting you phone.

Another Bluetooth device is not located

- Ensure Bluetooth feature is activated on your phone and the device you want to connect to.

- Ensure that your phone and the other Bluetooth device are within the maximum Bluetooth range (within 33 feet).

A connection is not established when you connect your phone to a PC

- Ensure that the USB cable you are using is compatible with your device.
- Ensure that you have the proper drivers/apps installed and updated on your PC.

Audio quality is poor

- When you are in an area with a weak or poor reception, you may lose reception. Try moving to another area and then try again.

Phone does not ring out

- Press/Slide the silent/ring button.

- Check if **Do Not Disturb** (see page 170) is enabled. If Do Not Disturb is enabled, your phone may not ring out.

Safety Precautions

A. To prevent electric shock, fire, and explosion:

1. Do not use damaged power cords or plugs, or loose electrical sockets.
2. Do not touch the power cord with a wet hand.
3. Do not bend or damage the power cord.
4. Do not short-circuit the charger.
5. Do not use your phone during thunderstorm.
6. Do not dispose your phone by putting it in fire.

B. Follow all safety warnings and regulations when using your device in restricted areas.

C. Comply with all safety warnings and regulations regarding mobile device usage while operating a vehicle.

D. Proper care and use of your phone

1. Do not use or store your phone in hot or cold areas. It is recommended to use your device at temperature from 5^0C to 35^0C.
2. Do not put your phone near magnetic fields.
3. Do not use camera flash close to eyes of people or pets because it can cause temporary loss of vision or damage the eyes.
4. Avoid disturbing others when using your phone in public.
5. Keep your phone away from small children because they may mistakenly damage it. It may look like a toy to them.

Just Before You Go (Please Read!)

Although I have put in tremendous efforts into writing this guide,
I am confident that I have not said it all.

I have no doubt believing that I have not written everything possible
about this device.

Therefore, I want you to do me a favor.

If you will like to know how to perform a task that is not included in
this guide, please let me know by sending me an email at
pharmibrahimguides@gmail.com. I will try as much as possible to
reply you as soon as I can.

You may also visit my author's page at

www.amazon.com/author/pharmibrahim

And please don't forget to follow me when you visit my author's
page, just click or tap on **Follow** button located below the profile
picture.

Made in the USA
Middletown, DE
24 May 2018